TEACHINGS FROM TIBET

Teachings from Tibet

Guidance from Great Lamas

EDITED BY Nicholas Ribush

LAMA YESHE WISDOM ARCHIVE • BOSTON
LamaYeshe.com

A non-profit charitable organization for the benefit of all sentient beings and an
affiliate of the Foundation for the Preservation of the Mahayana Tradition. fpmt.org

First published 2005
20,000 copies for free distribution
Second printing 2015, 5,000 copies

Lama Yeshe Wisdom Archive
PO Box 636
Lincoln, MA 01773, USA

Library of Congress Cataloging-in-Publication Data

Teachings at Tushita.
  Teachings from Tibet : guidance from great lamas /
edited by Nicholas Ribush.
    pages cm
  Previously published as: Teachings at Tushita. New Delhi :
Mahayana Publications, 1981.
  Includes bibliographical references.
  Summary: "A collection of teachings on all aspects of Buddhism
by various great lamas, given in India (mainly at Tushita Mahayana
Meditation Centre) and Nepal in the 1970s and 1980s, with
an introductory overview of the path to enlightenment by the editor"
— Provided by publisher.
  ISBN 978-1-891868-15-3
  1. Buddhism—Tibet Region—Doctrines. I. Ribush, Nicholas,
editor of compilation. II. Title.
  BQ4165.T43 2015
  294.3'420423—dc23
                                            2015001515
  ISBN 978-1-891868-15-3

10 9 8 7 6 5 4 3 2

Cover photograph by Pete from a thangka by Peter Iseli,
courtesy Nalanda Monastery, France.
Back cover drawing by Kyabje Trijang Rinpoche, 1972.

♻ Printed in the USA with environmental mindfulness on 30% PCW
recycled paper. The following resources have been saved: 17 trees, 515 lbs.
of solid waste, 7,681 gallons of water, 1,416 lbs. of greenhouse gases
and 7 million BTUs of energy.

CONTENTS

Publisher's Acknowledgments

W<small>E ARE EXTREMELY GRATEFUL</small> to our friends and supporters who have made it possible for the L<small>AMA</small> Y<small>ESHE</small> W<small>ISDOM</small> A<small>RCHIVE</small> to both exist and function, especially Lama Yeshe and Lama Zopa Rinpoche, whose kindness is impossible to repay. We have acknowledged the many people who have worked to develop the A<small>RCHIVE</small> over the years and who have contributed financially both in our previous publications and online and take this opportunity to thank them again for their indispensable assistance. In particular, our sustaining supporters and members make it possible for us to accomplish our aims, so thank you all once more.

If you, dear reader, would like to join this noble group of open-hearted altruists by contributing to the production of more free books by Lama Yeshe or Lama Zopa Rinpoche or to any other aspect of the L<small>AMA</small> Y<small>ESHE</small> W<small>ISDOM</small> A<small>RCHIVE</small>'s work, please contact us to find out how.

A NOTE ON HOW THIS BOOK CAME ABOUT

Back in the 1970s and '80s, most of the great lamas to leave Tibet were still alive and teaching. Those of us who had the good fortune to be in India and Nepal at that time were able to benefit by sitting at their feet, drinking in the nectar of their holy speech. It was a wonderful time.

Many of the teachings in this book were given at Tushita Mahayana Meditation Center, New Delhi, which, at Lama Yeshe's request, I established in 1977 and directed until 1983. They were originally published in a volume called *Teachings at Tushita* (New

Delhi: Mahayana Publications, 1981), which I co-edited with Glenn H. Mullin. I therefore acknowledge here Glenn's kind, if indirect, contribution to this book—they were all re-edited for the first edition of *Teachings from Tibet* (Boston: LYWA, 2005), with many valuable editorial suggestions from Linda Gatter. Gordon McDougall has made many excellent suggestions for improving on that, and I thank him for his contributions to this, the second edition of *Teachings from Tibet.*

Two of His Holiness the Dalai Lama's teachings contained herein were published in a souvenir booklet produced for Tushita's Second Dharma Celebration, November 1982, the first at which His Holiness spoke.

Three of the others are from unpublished manuscripts that I carried around for nearly thirty years, waiting for the right moment. This book was it. Please see the notes accompanying the author photos for details of the provenance of the teachings in this volume.

Nicholas Ribush

Through the merit of having contributed to the spread of the Buddha's teachings for the sake of all sentient beings, may our benefactors and their families and friends have long and healthy lives, all happiness, and may all their Dharma wishes be instantly fulfilled.

EDITOR'S INTRODUCTION
AN OUTLINE OF THE PATH TO ENLIGHTENMENT

THE BUDDHA TAUGHT so that beings would be happy and satisfied. Having attained the ultimate happiness of enlightenment himself, out of love and compassion for each sentient being he wanted to share his experience with them all. But he could not transplant his realizations into the minds of others, remove their suffering by hand or wash away their ignorance with water—he could only teach them to develop their minds for themselves, as he had done. Thus he showed the path to enlightenment.

THE NATURE OF THE MIND

There are two kinds of being with mind: buddhas and sentient beings. Buddhas were once sentient beings, but through engaging in and completing the practice of Dharma, they fully purified their minds of both gross and subtle obscurations and attained enlightenment, or buddhahood.

There are also two kinds of sentient being: those beyond cyclic existence and those within. Those beyond cyclic existence have purified their minds of the gross obscurations but not the subtle. Sentient beings within cyclic existence are suffering from both levels of obscuration and are under the control of the disturbing negative minds (delusions) and their imprints on the consciousness—*karma*.

The mind, or consciousness, is formless, just like empty space—it has no shape or color. But unlike empty space, this formless mind also has the property of awareness, the ability to perceive objects.

Additionally, the mind is impermanent, that is, changing from moment to moment. All impermanent phenomena are the products of causes, thus so is the mind—it does not arise from nothing. Furthermore, since effects must be similar in nature to their principal causes, the principal cause of the mind must also be a formless entity able to perceive objects and not some material substance such as the brain.

In other words, the mind proceeds from a previous state of mind; each thought moment is preceded by a prior thought moment and there has never been a first. Moreover, each being's mind comes from its own previous continuity and not from another mind, such as some "cosmic consciousness" or the minds of one's parents. Hence, each individual's mind is beginningless. And just as physical energy never goes out of existence, disappearing into nothingness, so too does mental energy continue forever; only its state changes.

HOW IS IT POSSIBLE TO ATTAIN ENLIGHTENMENT?

The mind is also different from empty space in that it has clear light nature. Our mind is like a mirror smeared with filth—its clear light nature is polluted by our delusions. However, just as the adventitious filth is not inextricably mixed with the potentially pure, clear mirror beneath, similarly, our delusions are not one with the mind. And just like an appropriate method, such as washing with soap and water, will clean the mirror; the right way to purify the mind of the delusions and their impressions, the subtle obscurations, is to practice Dharma. This results in the ultimate happiness of enlightenment and, since the minds of all sentient beings have clear light nature, all have the potential to become buddhas. The difficulty lies in finding the opportunity to practice Dharma and the interest in doing so.

THIS PRECIOUS HUMAN REBIRTH

Even if we have the opportunity to practice and the interest in doing so, we have to be taught how. Finding a perfectly qualified teacher is the most important thing in life, and once we have found this teacher we must follow him or her correctly—this is the root of the path to enlightenment.

Sentient beings in cyclic existence are of six types: those in the three lower realms—hell beings, hungry ghosts and animals—and those in the three upper realms—humans, "non-gods" (Skt: *asura*, sometimes called titans or demi-gods) and gods (Skt: *sura*). There are also countless beings in the intermediate state, about to be born into one of these six realms.

The sentient beings in the three lower realms cannot practice Dharma because they are oppressed by the heavy sufferings of ignorance, deprivation and pain. In the three upper realms, only humans can hope to practice Dharma—the suras and asuras are too distracted by either the enjoyment of high sense pleasures or fighting over them.

Even among human beings it is extremely difficult to find the freedom and circumstances to practice perfectly. Most are born at a time or in a place where there are neither teachers nor teachings. Even when born at an opportune time or place there will be either personal or environmental hindrances to meditation. If, upon reflection, we find ourselves with the perfect chance to practice Dharma, we should rejoice and enthusiastically make the most of our precious opportunity.

As Dharma practitioners, the least we can do is strive for the happiness of future lives, that is, rebirth in the upper realms. If we are wiser, we shall try to attain the everlasting bliss of *nirvana*, liberation from the whole of cyclic existence. And the wisest among us will realize that we have a chance to reach the ultimate goal of enlightenment for the benefit of all sentient beings and will set our mind on that alone. Every single moment of our precious human lives gives us the opportunity to purify eons of negative karma and take a giant step toward enlightenment by engaging in the profound practices of the Mahayana path. Wasting even a second of this life is an incalculable loss.

How do we waste our lives? By following the attachment that clings to the happiness of just this life. Practicing Dharma means renouncing this life, that is, the happiness of this life.

All sentient beings want happiness and do not want suffering, but desire alone is insufficient for us to accomplish our goals. Most of us do not know that happiness and suffering are the result of both principal and secondary causes. We recognize the secondary, or contributory, causes—such as food, drink, cold, heat, other sense objects and environmental conditions—but consider these to be the true causes of happiness and misery. Thus most of us are outward-looking and materialistic in our pursuit of fulfillment.

However, principal causes, mental imprints—karma—are what determine whether we shall experience happiness or suffering when we come into contact with a particular sense object. If we want to be happy all the time, under any circumstances, we have to fill our mind with positive karma and completely eradicate the negative. It is only through practicing Dharma that we can do all this, and practicing Dharma means first and foremost renouncing this life. All other practices are built on this foundation.

True Dharma practitioners do not care whether this life is happy or not—they are far more forward-looking than that—and just through this sincere change in attitude alone, they experience much more happiness in this life than do most others. Furthermore, they create much positive karma, which brings better and happier future lives, and liberation from samsara. Those who work for this life alone rarely experience contentment, create much negative karma and suffer in many lifetimes to come.

Simply desiring a better future life is not enough: we have to create the cause of an upper rebirth consciously and with great effort, by practicing morality. And to receive a perfect human rebirth, with its eight freedoms and ten richnesses for Dharma practice, we must also practice generosity and the other perfections of patience, enthusiastic perseverance, concentration and wisdom. Finally, all these causes have to be linked to the desired result by stainless prayer.

Hence it is easy to see why a perfect human rebirth is so hard to get—it is extremely difficult to create its cause. One virtually has to have a perfect human rebirth in order to create the cause for another.

IMPERMANENCE AND DEATH

We are certain to die but have no idea when death will come. Each day could be our last, yet we act as if we were going to live forever. This attitude prevents us from practicing Dharma at all or else leads us to postpone our practice or to practice sporadically or impurely. We create negative karma without a second thought, rationalizing that it can always be purified later. And when death does arrive, we die with much sorrow and regret, seeing clearly but too late how we lost our precious chance.

By meditating on the certainty of death, how our lives are continuously running out and how the time of death is uncertain, we shall be sure to practice Dharma and to practice it right now. When we meditate further on how material possessions, worldly power, friends and family and even our most cherished body cannot help us at the time of death, we shall be sure to practice only Dharma.

Our situation is this: we have been born human with all the conditions of a perfect human rebirth, but so far we have spent our lives almost exclusively in the creation of negative karma. If we were to die right now—and where is the guarantee that we won't— we would definitely be reborn in one of the three lower realms, from which it is nearly impossible to escape. But ignorance prevents us from recognizing the urgency and danger of our position, and instead of seeking an object of refuge, we relax and spend our time creating only more negative karma.

REFUGE

When we have a problem we usually take refuge in sense objects: when we are hungry, we eat food; when thirsty, we drink something;

when it's raining we jump under an umbrella. These things may help solve such superficial problems temporarily, but what we really need is a solution to our deepest, most chronic problems: the ignorance, attachment and aversion so firmly rooted in our mind—the source of all suffering.

When we are seriously ill we rely on a doctor to make the diagnosis and prescribe the appropriate medication and on a nurse to help us take it. We are now suffering from the most serious illness there is, the disease of the delusions. The supreme physician, the Buddha, has already made the diagnosis and prescribed the medicine, the Dharma; it is up to us to take it. The Sangha, the monastic community, help us to put into practice the Dharma teachings we have received.

FOLLOWING KARMA

What does it mean to take the medicine of Dharma, to put the teachings into practice? The Buddha has shown us the nature of reality; now it's up to us to try to live in accordance with it by observing the law of karma, cause and effect. Positive karma brings happiness; negative karma brings suffering. Actions of body, speech and mind leave positive or negative imprints on the consciousness, which are like seeds planted in the ground. Under suitable conditions they ripen and produce their results.

The positivity or negativity of a particular action is determined primarily by the motivation behind it and its effect—mainly the former—not by its outward appearance. Basically, actions motivated by the desire for the happiness of just this life are negative, whereas those motivated by the desire for happiness in future lives, liberation or enlightenment are, if appropriate, positive. Since we have neither the insight to detect the true motivation for our actions nor the clairvoyance to determine their effects, the Buddha laid down a fundamental code of moral conduct for beginners: the ten negative actions to avoid. These are known as the ten nonvirtues: three of body (killing, stealing and sexual misconduct), four of speech (lying, slandering, speaking harshly and gossiping) and three of mind (covetousness, malice and wrong views). In practice, we must avoid creating negative actions and purify the imprints that those of the past have left on our mindstreams. We must also develop whatever positive tendencies we have and acquire those that are missing. In this way we gradually develop our mind to perfection and experience ever-increasing happiness as we do.

RENUNCIATION OF SUFFERING

The happiness we experience in samsara is dangerous because we get attached to it very easily. However, while it appears to be happiness, it isn't true happiness: it never lasts, always changes into suffering and, in fact, is merely a lessening of the suffering we were just experiencing. Just as we feel aversion to obvious sufferings such as pain, illness and worry and want to be free of them, so should we renounce transient pleasures and even upper rebirths and strive single-pointedly to escape from samsara. The fully renounced mind, the first of the three principal teachings of Buddhism, is that which yearns for liberation day and night. It is the main source of energy for those who seek nirvana and serves as the basis for their development of perfect concentration and right view of reality as they proceed toward their goal of arhatship.

WORKING FOR OTHERS

Equanimity

But it is not enough to strive simply for our own personal liberation. We are the same as all other sentient beings in wanting all happiness and freedom from even the tiniest suffering, and it is selfish and cruel to desire and strive for everlasting bliss and perfect peace for ourselves alone. The most intelligent of us will see that until each and every sentient being has finally found the highest possible happiness, our individual responsibility to others has not been fulfilled. Why responsibility? Because all our past, present and future happiness up to and including enlightenment depends on all other sentient beings without exception. It is our duty to repay this kindness.

The first hindrance we must overcome is our chronic habit of feeling attached to some sentient beings, averse to others and indifferent toward the rest. As our ego—the wrong conception of the way we exist—makes us feel "I" very strongly, we strive for our own self-happiness, shy away from whatever we deem unpleasant and remain indifferent to the rest. We associate various sense objects with these feelings, and when these objects happen to be other beings, we label them "friend," "enemy" and "stranger." As a result, we become strongly attached to and try to help our friends; hate and try to harm our enemies; and avoid and ignore the vast majority of other sentient beings—strangers we feel to be totally unconnected with either our happiness or our problems. Therefore, we have to train our mind to feel equanimity toward all sentient beings, to feel them all equally deserving of our efforts to help them find the happiness they seek.

Even in this life, the present friend to whom we are attached and try to help has not always been our friend. Earlier on we had no idea of his (or her) existence and, as he neither helped nor hindered our pursuit of happiness, we categorized that person as a "stranger." When later he somehow or other gratified our ego, we began to regard him as useful, as a "friend," and thus fostered his attention by being nice to him and doing whatever we could to look good in his eyes, concealing our faults in the process.

However, the friendly relations between the two of us—maintained by a certain amount of effort and a good deal of deception on both sides—will not last. Sooner or later one of us will do something to upset the other or get bored with the relationship. Then the other person, who appeared so desirable, will start to become unattractive, someone to be avoided. Gradually, or even suddenly, the relationship will deteriorate and we shall become "enemies." Of course, this doesn't always happen, but all of us have had experiences like it.

Hence, the labels of "friend," "enemy" and "stranger" we apply to others are very temporary and not based on some ultimate aspect of reality to be found in the other. They are projected by our ego on the basis of whether that person seems useful for our own happiness, causes us problems or does not appear to be involved one way or the other.

In some previous lives our best friends of this life have been our worst enemies. The same is true of our enemies of today—in previous lives they were parents, friends and strangers too. As these ever-changing samsaric relationships are beginningless, we can see that each sentient being has functioned as our friend, enemy and stranger, taking each role an infinite number of times. Thus all sentient beings are equal in this way, and none is more deserving of our help than any other, irrespective of the tunnel vision of our present view. Furthermore, as long as we remain in samsara these relationships will continue to change. Therefore, there is no reason to be attached to our friends, who will soon become harm-giving enemies, or to hate our enemies, who are sure to become beloved friends. By fully opening our mind and seeing things in the broadest possible perspective we shall see all sentient beings as they really are—equal—and all will be attractive and dear.

Seeing all sentient beings as mother

If all sentient beings have been our enemy, perhaps we should try to harm them all equally! While it may be true that, out of ignorance and anger, they have all hurt us in the past, their kindness far exceeds their cruelty. Through depending equally on every single sentient being, and only through this, we receive the sublime, everlasting happiness of enlightenment. But even in a worldly way has each sentient being been kind—each has been our mother, and not just once.

Every sentient being has had an infinite number of rebirths, but our mother of this life has not been our mother in each of our previous lives—usually we were not even born together in the same realm or with the same type of body. Also, there is no samsaric body or realm that has not been experienced by any sentient being and no time that sentient beings first began to be mothers.

Thus, each sentient being has been our mother an infinite number of times and, constantly keeping this fact in mind, we should try to see each one as our mother. Imagine that our mother has been caught in a fire and burnt beyond recognition—we know it's her but can't tell by looking; it's the same stream of consciousness and we feel incredible compassion for her unbearable suffering. Similarly, if we do the above analytical meditation properly, when we see insects, for example, we'll feel that they are our mother of a previous time—it is the same stream of consciousness—but having to undergo the great suffering of being trapped in such an unfortunate body. Hence love and compassion will arise whenever we see any sentient being.

A mother's kindness

Why do we more easily feel love and compassion for our mother? Because normally, our love and compassion are impure, partial. They are not directed equally at all, only toward those who help us, our "friends." And our mother is the best friend of all.

We must meditate on just how kind our mother has been. She happily underwent many difficulties to bear us, to give us this precious human body; she fed us and protected us from harm when we were helpless; she taught us to speak, walk and look after ourselves; she ensured we had a good education; she provided us with the necessities and enjoyments of life. She has always put our welfare ahead of hers: who else has been so kind? The more we recollect the kindness of the mother, the greater will be our affection for her—this is natural. The more we recognize other sentient beings as mother, the greater will be our affection for them all. And the greater will be the thought of repaying their kindness.

Repaying kindness

Wanting to repay others' kindness is also a natural and positive emotion, and the repayment should at least equal the kindness shown. Since we receive enlightenment from each and every mother sentient being, it is our responsibility to see that each also receives it.

Cherishing others

The greatest hindrance to enlightenment is the self-cherishing mind, which puts our own happiness ahead of everybody else's and causes us to act accordingly. Every personal problem we have ever experienced has come from this; so too has every interpersonal problem, from the smallest argument among children to wars between nations. The more we think about it the more we shall see that the self-cherishing mind is the most dangerous thing that exists. Yet it can be destroyed and replaced by the mind that cherishes others, putting ourselves last of all. This is the greatest mind we can generate—it gives rise to the state of enlightenment. We must cultivate the mind that cherishes others more than ourselves.

From seeing that no sentient being, ourselves included, wants or deserves happiness and freedom from suffering more than any other, a feeling of equality arises. As the desire for these ends is the same, why should we act as if our happiness were more important than anybody else's? There can be no logical justification for such an attitude. Moreover, if all suffering—from the smallest to the greatest—arises from the self-cherishing mind, surely we should wait not a moment longer to destroy it completely. Thinking like this, we engage in the practice of exchanging self for others.

Exchanging self for others is not a physical practice. It means that so far, since beginningless time, we have been going around harboring the thought deep in our hearts, "My happiness is the most important thing there is." It may not be conscious, but its presence is reflected in our actions. So now, instead of putting ourselves first we put ourselves last: "My happiness is the least important of all." In this way we can destroy the self-cherishing mind.

The practice of taking and giving

We also practice the meditation of taking the suffering of others upon ourselves and giving them all happiness. Visualizing all sentient beings in the three realms undergoing their respective sufferings, we inhale all those sufferings in the form of black smoke, which smashes the self-cherishing conception at our hearts. When we exhale we send out pure white light, which reaches all sentient beings, bringing them everything they want and need, temporally and spiritually—all the realizations of the path, from devotion to the spiritual master to enlightenment. At the end, we visualize all sentient beings in the aspect of buddhas.

Arising from this meditation we may feel that it was of no use—all the sentient beings are still suffering, just as they were when we started it. But each time we do this meditation we damage our self-cherishing mind and move much closer to enlightenment.

GENERATING BODHICITTA

We should wish sincerely and pray from the bottom of our heart: "May all sentient beings free themselves from all suffering and ignorance and find the perfect bliss of enlightenment." Feeling it our responsibility to see them do so, we should vow to bring about each sentient being's enlightenment ourselves, and understand what we must do to fulfill this obligation. In our present condition we can't even guarantee ourselves temporal happiness—how can we hope to bring others to perfect bliss? Only a buddha can lead others to buddhahood, therefore, each of us must reach that state in order to help others get there. Thus we determine, "For the sole purpose of enlightening all sentient beings I shall reach enlightenment myself." When this thought becomes a realization underlying our every action it is called *bodhicitta*.

Bodhicitta is the most precious mind we can strive for—it is the principal cause of enlightenment. It is the most virtuous mind—with bodhicitta we can obliterate vast accumulations of negative karma and create huge amounts of merit. It is the most beneficial mind—when we have bodhicitta, whatever we do helps all other sentient beings in the highest way, and when through it we have attained enlightenment, we work as buddhas for the enlightenment of all sentient beings. To fulfill our vow of enlightening all sentient beings we must first receive bodhicitta by training our mind in all the preceding meditations, starting from devotion to our spiritual teacher.

To help us in this we take the sixty-four bodhisattva vows from a fully qualified teacher and train ourselves in the six perfections of giving, morality, patience, enthusiastic perseverance, concentration and wisdom.

EMPTINESS: THE RIGHT VIEW OF REALITY

Just as those who seek nirvana must develop perfect concentration and the right view of reality, so too must trainee bodhisattvas. How? By practicing the latter two perfections.[1] On the prerequisite basis of perfect moral conduct—impeccable observation of the law of karma and the vows we have taken—we develop single-pointed concentration. Then, having first gained conceptual insight into emptiness, the ultimate nature of all phenomena, we use our perfect concentration to gain direct, non-conceptual insight into the ultimate nature of our own mind. With this achieved, we gradually develop insight into the nature of all other phenomena.

Practicing all the analytical meditations of the graduated path

---

[1] See Gelek Rimpoche's "Developing Single-pointed Concentration," p. 169, and Geshe Ngawang Dhargyey's "In Search of the Self," p. 179.

in their correct sequence brings us the three major realizations: the fully renounced mind, bodhicitta and right view, the wisdom realizing emptiness. Thus we are qualified to enter the quick path to enlightenment, the Vajrayana.

TANTRA: THE HIGHEST PATH

There are two ways of reaching enlightenment, one prolonged, the other fast. Practitioners of the Paramitayana, the perfection vehicle, take three countless great eons to attain the goal. Lifetime after lifetime, bodhisattvas traveling this path take rebirth in samsara for the benefit of all sentient beings, gradually approaching buddhahood through practicing the six perfections and other methods, sacrificing their lives for the enlightenment of others. We see some examples of this in the stories of Guru Shakyamuni Buddha's previous lives, the *Jataka Tales*.

For other bodhisattvas, this is too slow. Those who are filled with compassion for the suffering of other sentient beings—who feel unbearable at the thought of others suffering for even a second longer, who feel other sentient beings' suffering as their own, as if they themselves had been plunged into boiling oil, who want to put an immediate end to samsara, who are fully qualified physically and mentally—have been shown the supreme path of tantra by the Buddha.

However, because the tantric path to enlightenment is the quickest, it is also the most difficult to follow. The consequences of mistakes made by tantric practitioners are far more serious than those made by followers of lower paths. Thus few beings have the ability or opportunity to enter this path.

As ever, the most important thing is to have a fully qualified spiritual master. Having established a guru-disciple relationship, it is then crucial that the student follow his or her teacher correctly. The vajra guru gives students initiations, tantric vows and teachings on the two stages of tantra—the generation and completion stages.

Under his guidance, disciples practice the special techniques of tantra and, for the rare and most fortunate few, it is possible to gain enlightenment in this very life; that is, they enter and complete the Vajrayana path in a single lifetime.

This, in brief, is an outline of the path to enlightenment (*lam-rim*), as taught and followed by most of the Tibetan schools of Buddhism. They vary in their modes of presentation and in the study and meditation techniques employed, but their similarities are much greater than their differences.

A Lamp for the Path
to Enlightenment[2]

Commentary by Khunu Lama Rinpoche

COURTESY JÜRGEN MANSHARDT

[2] For a translation of the root text, see appendix 2.

B EFORE LISTENING TO this teaching, first generate bodhicitta, thinking, "I want to receive enlightenment for the benefit of all mother sentient beings." In other words, before listening to teachings, it is necessary to think of, to remember, all mother sentient beings.

The subject today is *Lam-drön, A Lamp for the Path to Enlightenment*, which was written in Tibet by the great Atisha (Dipamkara Shrijnana), who was born about the year 982 in northeast India as the son of a Bengali king.

ATISHA AND THE LATER SPREAD OF DHARMA IN TIBET[3]

Buddhadharma had already been established in Tibet before Atisha's arrival there, but an evil king called Langdarma (Udumtsen), who was said to have horns growing from his head, hated the Dharma and caused it to degenerate in Tibet. But even though the teachings had been corrupted, they still existed—just not as purely as before. It took about sixty years to restore the teachings to their original purity in what became known as the later spreading of the Dharma in Tibet.

How that happened was that in western Tibet, in the kingdom of Gugé, there lived a Tibetan king, Lha Lama Yeshe Ö, and his nephew, Jangchub Ö. They decided to invite a learned and realized teacher from the great Indian monastery of Vikramashila to spread Dharma in Tibet. When they investigated to see who was the most learned and realized person there, they discovered that Atisha would be by far the best one to invite.

But before Lha Lama Yeshe Ö could request Atisha to come from Vikramashila to Tibet, he needed to find gold to make a proper offering, so went to a place called Garlog in search of it. However,

[3] For a long version of this story, see Pabongka Rinpoche, *Liberation in the Palm of Your Hand*, 27–52.

before he could accomplish his mission, the ruler of Garlog threw him in prison, where he died. In that way, Lha Lama Yeshe Ö sacrificed his life to bring Atisha to Tibet.

Then his nephew, Jangchub Ö, sent emissaries to India to invite Atisha to Tibet. When he finally met Atisha, he explained how the Dharma had degenerated during Langdarma's rule and how correct teachings no longer existed in Tibet, and requested Atisha to give the Tibetan people fundamental teachings on refuge, bodhicitta and so forth because they were so ignorant. Therefore, Atisha wrote the precious teaching, *A Lamp for the Path to Enlightenment*. This text is based on the *prajnaparamita* teachings of Shakyamuni Buddha and is the source of not only all the Gelug lam-rim teachings but also those of the other main schools of Tibetan Buddhism— Nyingma, Kagyü and Sakya—which all practice the graduated path to enlightenment and quote it in their teachings.

After generating bodhicitta, as above, our main task is to attain enlightenment. Now, even though we might think that life in samsara is pleasant, it's not. There is no true pleasure in samsara. Enlightenment can be attained only through the practice of Dharma. Therefore, we should all practice Dharma.

In terms of teachings in general, there are two types: Buddhadharma and the teachings of the outsiders,[4] which are based on mistaken beliefs, understandings opposite to those of Buddhadharma. By following such non-Buddhist teachings, you can be born anywhere from the lower realms to the peak of samsara, the highest of the four formless realms, but you can never escape from suffering.

Within the Buddhadharma, there are also two divisions: Hinayana and Mahayana. By following Hinayana teachings, you can escape from samsara but you cannot attain enlightenment. To attain enlightenment, you have to practice Mahayana teachings. Within the Mahayana there are the teachings spoken by the Buddha himself and those written later by his learned followers, the eminent Indian

---

[4] Skt: *tirthika;* Tib: *mu-teg-pa.* See Jeffrey Hopkins, *Meditation on Emptiness,* 320-21.

pandits, including the six ornaments and the two supremes,[5] and the great Tibetan masters.

The teaching we are discussing here, then, is that written by the learned pandit Dipamkara Shrijnana, the *Lam-drön*. What is it about? It comes from Maitreya's *Ornament for Clear Realization (Abhisamayalamkara)* and explains the three levels of teaching: the paths of practitioners of small, medium and higher capacity, especially the latter.

VERSE-BY-VERSE COMMENTARY

The text opens with the title of this teaching in Sanskrit, which in Tibetan is *Jang-chub lam-gyi drön-ma*. This is followed by homage to Manjushri.

1. The first verse includes three things. First there is homage to the Triple Gem: the buddhas of the three times, the oral teachings and realization of them, and the Sangha—those who have received the unshakable, or noble, path. Second, he mentions that his pure disciple, Jangchub Ö, requested him to give this teaching. Third, he makes the promise, or vow, to write this teaching, this lamp for the path to enlightenment, the *Lam-drön*.

2. In the second verse, Atisha explains what he's going to write about: the graduated paths of the persons of small, medium and higher capacity, or capability. These are also the paths that Lama Tsongkhapa explains in his short, middle-length and great lam-rim teachings—the graduated paths of these three types of practitioner.

3. Of the three levels of follower, Atisha first explains the graduated path of those of small capability. Such people think, "I don't care what suffering or happiness I experience in this life; I must avoid

---

[5] These are the great Indian scholars Nagarjuna, Aryadeva, Asanga, Vasubandhu, Dharmakirti and Dignaga, and Shakyaprabha and Gunaprabha.

rebirth in the lower realms and attain an upper rebirth." With this in mind, practitioners of small capability abstain from negative actions and practice virtue.

4. Persons of medium capability develop aversion to not only the sufferings of the three lower realms but also to those of the three upper realms—to the whole of samsara. Such practitioners abstain from negative actions in order to free themselves from samsara, without much concern for other sentient beings.

5. Who, then, are the beings of higher capability? They are those who, having understood their own suffering, take it as an example of the suffering that other beings are also experiencing and generate the great wish of wanting to put an end to the suffering of all sentient beings.

6-11. There are six preparatory practices. First, visualize the merit field and make offerings. Then kneel down with your hands in prostration and take refuge in the Triple Gem. After that, generate love for other sentient beings by thinking of the sufferings of death, old age, sickness and rebirth as well as the three sufferings and the general suffering of samsara. In that way, generate bodhicitta.

12-17. It is necessary to generate the aspiration to attain enlightenment, and the benefits of doing so have been explained in the sutra called *Array of Trunks*. Atisha also quotes three verses from another sutra, the *Sutra Requested by Viradatta*, to further explain the benefits of bodhicitta.

18-19. There are two types of bodhicitta, conventional and ultimate.[6] Within the category of conventional there are two further

---

[6] Conventional bodhicitta is the wish to attain enlightenment for the sake of all sentient beings and ultimate bodhicitta is the realization of emptiness with a bodhicitta motivation.

divisions, aspirational bodhicitta—wanting to receive enlighten-ment for the benefit of other sentient beings, thinking, "Without my receiving enlightenment, I cannot enlighten others"—and engaging bodhicitta, actually following the bodhisattva's path by taking the bodhisattva precepts and engaging in the actions of a bodhisattva, thinking, "In order to engage in positive actions and avoid negative ones, I am going to practice the six perfections."

20-21. The teachings explain that in order to practice engaging bodhicitta, we should take the bodhisattva ordination, but in order to do so we should hold one of the seven levels of *pratimoksha* ordi-nation, such as *gelong, gelongma, getsul, getsulma* and so forth.[7] Ideally, then, we should hold one of these fundamental ordinations before taking the bodhisattva vow, but the learned ones say that in general, those who avoid negative karma and create virtuous actions can actualize bodhicitta, even if they don't hold any pra-timoksha precepts.

22. Aspirational bodhicitta can be generated without dependence upon a lama, but engaging bodhicitta depends on a lama. To find a lama from whom we can take the bodhisattva vow, we have to know the qualifications of such a lama.

23-24. First, the lama should know all about the ordination and how to bestow it. Furthermore, he should himself be living in the bodhisattva ordination and have compassion for the disciple. That's the kind of lama we need to find from whom to take the ordination. But what if we can't find a perfect lama like that? Atisha then goes on to explain what, in that case, we should do.

25-31. The *Ornament of Manjushri's Buddha Land Sutra* explains how, long ago, Manjushri generated bodhicitta. This is what we

<hr/>

[7] See the Dalai Lama, *Illuminating the Path to Enlightenment*, 123.

can do. Visualize the merit field and all the buddhas and, in their presence, generate bodhicitta, the intention to attain enlightenment. Then promise, "I invite all sentient beings as my guest to the sublime happiness of liberation and enlightenment. I will not get angry or harbor avarice, covetousness, jealousy and so forth. I will not harm other sentient beings in any way. I will live in pure discipline by avoiding all negative actions, even worldly desires and sense objects of attachment, such as attractive sounds and beautiful forms and so forth. I shall give up such things. As all the buddhas have followed pure moral conduct, so shall I.

"I will not try to receive enlightenment for myself alone. Even though it takes an endless amount of time to work for even one sentient being, I shall remain in samsara. I shall make pure the impure realms of sentient beings, places where there are thorns, rocks and ugly mountains. I shall also purify my three doors of body, speech and mind and keep them pure. From now on, I will create no more negative actions."

32-35. The best way to keep our three doors pure is to generate aspirational bodhicitta, engage in the practice of bodhicitta and follow the path to enlightenment. This depends on observing the three levels of moral conduct—the pratimoksha, bodhisattva and tantric vows. If we do this properly, we can complete the two collections of merit and transcendent wisdom.

One thing that really helps us complete these two collections is the ability to foresee the future; therefore, we should try to acquire clairvoyance. Without it, we are like a baby bird whose wings are undeveloped and has not yet grown feathers and remains stuck in its nest, unable to fly. Without clairvoyance, we cannot work for other sentient beings.

36-37. A person who has achieved the psychic power to foresee the future can create more merit in a day than a person without this ability can create in a hundred years. Therefore, to complete the collections of merit and transcendent wisdom quickly, it is necessary to acquire the psychic power to see past, present and future.

38. In order to do this, it is necessary to achieve single-pointed concentration. For this, we must understand the details of the method of attaining samadhi, such as the nine stages, the six powers and the four mental engagements.[8]

39. In order to practice samadhi meditation properly, we must ensure that the conditions are perfect. If they are not, then even though we try practicing it hard for even a thousand years, we'll never achieve it. Therefore we should find the perfect environment, remain quiet and avoid having to do work such as healing the ill and making astrological predictions—any activity that keeps us busy.

40. The way to meditate to attain single-pointed concentration is to focus our mind on a virtuous object, such as an image of the Buddha. We visualize such an image in front of us and simply concentrate on that. As we focus our mind on the object again and again, we'll be able to hold it for increasingly greater periods of time, and through the continuity of such practice will eventually attain calm abiding and single-pointed concentration. Thus we will gain "higher seeing,"[9] the psychic power to see the future and so forth.

41-43. But that is not the point. Next we have to practice penetrative insight. Without it, our samadhi cannot remove our delusions. In order to eradicate our two levels of obscuration—the obscurations of delusion and the obscurations to knowledge, or omniscience—we must achieve the wisdom realizing the non-self-existence of the I. Doing so also depends upon achieving method, such as compassion and so forth. It's a mistake to practice only wisdom and not method. This can lead us to fall into individual liberation, or lower

---

[8] See the Dalai Lama, *Opening the Eye of New Awareness*, 53-66.
[9] Tib: *ngön-she*.

nirvana. Similarly, practicing only method and not wisdom is also a mistake and causes us to remain in samsara.

44-46. The Buddha taught that of the six perfections, the last of the six is the path of wisdom and the first five—giving, morality, patience, effort and concentration—are the path of method, or skillful means.[10] First, we should meditate on method, then on wisdom, then on both together. By practicing both together, we can receive enlightenment; by practicing the wisdom of selflessness alone, we cannot.

47-49. Realizing the five aggregates, the twelve sources and the eighteen constituents as empty of self-existence is recognized as higher wisdom.[11] There is existence and non-existence: there is no such thing as the production of the existent; nor is there such a thing as production of the non-existent. There is no such thing as production of both the existent and the non-existent; nor is there production of neither the existent nor the non-existent. That is one form of logic negating the production of both the existent and the non-existent. There is also another form of logic negating production of a thing from self, other, both or neither—the four extremes. The main thing to discover here is non-self-existence. That can be found through the first line of logical reasoning, which negates production of the existent and the non-existent, and through the second, which negates production of the four extremes.

50-51. It can also be discovered through a third line of reasoning that examines things to see whether they are one or many. These

---

[10] Skt: *upaya*; Tib: *thab*.

[11] The five aggregates are the psycho-physical constituents that make up a sentient being: form, feeling, discrimination, compositional factors and consciousness; the twelve sources (Skt: *ayatana*; Tib: *kye-che*) are the six consciousnesses (eye, ear etc.) and their six sources (form source, sound source etc.); the eighteen constituents (Skt: *dhatu*; Tib: *kham*) are the six sense powers, the six consciousnesses and their six objects.

lines of reasoning are elaborated by Nagarjuna in his *Seventy Stanzas on Emptiness* and in other texts, such as his *Treatise on the Middle Way.*

52-54. These things are explained in those texts, but here they are mentioned just for the purpose of practicing meditation. Meditating on the non-self-existence of the I and the non-self-existence of all other phenomena is meditation on *shunyata*, or emptiness. When the wisdom realizing emptiness analyzes the subject and the object, it cannot discover self-existence in either of those. Moreover, it cannot find self-existence in the wisdom of emptiness either. Thus, we realize the emptiness of even the wisdom of emptiness itself.

55-58. Since this world is created by superstition, or conceptuality,[12] if we eradicate the creator, superstition, we can attain liberation. The Buddha said that it is superstition that causes us to fall into the ocean of samsara. Therefore, that which is to be avoided is superstition, but the emptiness of superstition, which is like the sky, like empty space, is that which is to be practiced. By achieving this, we will be able to see the ultimate nature of existence. Therefore, the bodhisattvas' practice is to avoid superstition and thus to achieve the non-superstitious mind. Through the various different means of logic—by realizing the emptiness of the produced and of inherent existence—we can avoid superstition and achieve the wisdom of shunyata.

59. Then we can also attain the different levels of the path of preparation, the second of the five paths. We attain the four levels of this path and gradually the ten bodhisattva grounds as well. Finally, we attain the eleventh level, enlightenment itself.

60-67. Having realized shunyata, we can also gain the general realizations of tantra, such as the four powers of pacification, wrath,

[12] Tib: *nam-tog.*

control and increase, and other attainments, such as "accomplishing the good pot." Accomplishing the good pot means doing a particular meditation in retreat for a long time and, if we are successful, gaining the ability to just put our mouth to the opening of a pot and say something like "May I become the king of this country" and have our wish fulfilled.

Or we can gain the tantric power of the "eye medicine." If we accomplish this, just by applying a special ointment to our eye we can see precious substances such as gold, jewels and so forth even hundreds of miles beneath the surface of the earth; no matter how far away they are, we can see them.

Through the practice of tantra we can receive enlightenment without having to undergo many great austerities. The tantric way to enlightenment is through happiness; other paths to enlightenment are through hard, austere practice.

There are four different levels of tantra: Action, Performance, Yoga and Highest Yoga Tantra. First we have to receive initiation. In order to do so, we have to make material offerings, such as gold or even members of our family—a spouse or a sibling— and with great devotion request our guru to give us the initiation.[13] If he is pleased, out of his compassion he will then give us the initiation. Having taken it, we also receive the great fortune of being able to attain enlightenment and all the high realizations that come with it.

In Highest Yoga Tantra there are four different initiations: the vase, secret, transcendent wisdom and word initiations, the last being where the guru imparts clarification, or proof, through verbal explanation. However, the secret initiation should not be given to those living in ordination. If monks, for example, take the secret initiation, they have to leave the monastic order, because those who have taken the secret initiation are required to practice with a female consort. If they do these practices without first returning their ordination, they lose it, the consequence of which is rebirth in hell.

---

[13] These days, initiations seem a bit easier to come by.

To receive tantric commentaries, you first have to receive initiation. Without initiation, you cannot receive tantric teachings. You also cannot perform fire pujas[14] or give tantric teachings.

68. In the last verse, Atisha closes this text by describing himself as an elder,[15] a full monk who, in the first twelve years after taking ordination, did not create any moral falls; a senior full monk. He states that he has given this brief explanation on the steps of path at the request of his noble follower, Jangchub Ö.

CONCLUSION

Every lam-rim teaching ever written refers back to this text, *A Lamp for the Path*, irrespective of the Tibetan Buddhist tradition. What does the *Lamp* itself refer back to? That is to the Buddha's prajnaparamita teachings. In terms of prajnaparamita texts, there are elaborate, intermediate and short, but the author of all of them is the Buddha. Therefore, all lam-rim texts have their source in the teachings of the Buddha.

If you want to understand the lam-rim well, you should study it as extensively as possible. When you understand the lam-rim well, you will understand the *Lamp for the Path*. Once you do, you should teach it all over the world.

There are many aspects of the Mahayana tradition, but in general, it contains great knowledge. The main thing, however, the fundamental thing, is concern for others, working for others, benefiting others. Followers of the Hinayana are mainly concerned about only their own samsaric suffering—in order to escape it, they follow the path of the three higher trainings: higher conduct, higher concentration and higher wisdom. There are many ways to explain how the Mahayana is different from and higher than the Hinayana, but the

---

[14] Tib: *jin-sek.*
[15] Tib: *nä-tän.*

main difference is that Mahayana practitioners are more concerned with working for the welfare of others than their own.

People nowadays might think of helping other people, but Mahayana practitioners benefit not only other people but also suffering hell beings, pretas, animals and every other sentient being. There is not one sentient being who has not been our mother—all sentient beings have been our mother numberless times—therefore we *should* be concerned for their welfare, wanting them to become enlightened as quickly as possible. This, then, is the fundamental difference between the Hinayana and the Mahayana, this concern more for others than oneself, in particular, the wish to enlighten all sentient beings. That's what makes the difference.

It is excellent that you are studying the vast and profound teachings of the Mahayana, thinking about them, analyzing them intently, and you should continue to do so. In general, there are many religions and everyone thinks that the teaching of his or her own religion is the best. But just saying that one's own religion is the best doesn't prove it's the best; that doesn't mean anything. Therefore, simply saying that Buddhadharma is the best religion in the world doesn't make it so. However, there are many logical reasons you can use to *prove* that Buddhadharma is, in fact, the best.

For example, even accepting and practicing bodhicitta is very different from not accepting or practicing bodhicitta. Even in this, there's a big difference between Buddhism and other religions. Just the fact of the presence of the practice of bodhicitta shows that Buddhism is higher than other religions, that Buddhism is the best. But Buddhism also talks about dependent origination and emptiness; it explains dependent origination as it exists, right there. So, not only in conduct but also in view, Buddhism is very different from other religions and therefore the best. There are many ways to prove this.

Anyway, Buddhadharma is something that the more you study it, the deeper it becomes, the more profound you find it to be. This is a quality unique to Buddhadharma. With other teachings, the more you study them, the lighter they become.

If you have understood any of what I have taught here, keep it in mind and build upon it. When you have understood more, keep that as your foundation and build further upon that. In this way, your knowledge will continually increase. Then, like the sun rising, spread Dharma in the West.

There are many countries, such as Vietnam, where Buddhism existed for centuries, but none were like Tibet. In those countries there existed only one aspect of the Buddhadharma, not all; but in Tibet, all aspects of the teaching existed—Hinayana, Sutrayana and Vajrayana. In order to study all this, you should learn the Tibetan language, study its grammar, and follow your lama properly.

[Dedication prayers are made and then the monks and nuns try to make offerings to Rinpoche.]

Please, don't offer me anything. I have enough to eat and drink; that's all I need. The reason I have given you this teaching is not to receive something but for you to practice purely. I'm not building monasteries or making offerings to statues and so forth so I have no need for money. I accept offerings only when I lack something. When I have enough, I don't accept offerings, especially not from monks or nuns. My idea of wealth is different. Otherwise, teaching and taking money is a bit like making business. For now, I just want you to practice, but if things get bad and I don't have enough to eat or drink, then maybe I'll accept something.

Born in the Indo-Tibetan borderlands at the end of the nineteenth century, Khunu Lama Rinpoche Tenzin Gyaltsen (1894–1977) was revered by Tibetan Buddhists of all traditions because his life embodied the spiritual practice of compassion. Among his many students was His Holiness the Dalai Lama. His most famous written work is *Vast as the Heavens, Deep as the Sea: Verses in Praise of Bodhicitta* (Wisdom Publications, 1999). He gave this teaching to the monks and nuns of the International Mahayana Institute in Boudhanath, Nepal, 2 February 1975. It was translated by Lama Zopa Rinpoche.

SEEKING AN INNER REFUGE

His Holiness the Dalai Lama

The purpose of Buddhism

FROM THE BUDDHIST point of view, the minds of ordinary people are weak and distorted because of the delusions and emotional afflictions they carry within. As a result, they are unable to see things as they actually exist; what they see is a vision that is twisted and defined by their own emotional neuroses and preconceptions.

The purpose of Buddhism is to remove these distortions from the mind and thus facilitate valid perception. As long as we have not uprooted our delusions, our perception remains tainted; when we eradicate them we enter a state of always seeing reality as it is. Then, because our mind abides in perfect wisdom and liberation, our body and speech automatically course in wholesome ways. This benefits not only us but also others, in both this life and those that follow. Therefore, Buddhism is said to be a path not simply of faith but also one of reason and knowledge.

How to study Buddhism

Tibetans are fortunate to have been born into a society where spiritual knowledge was both available and highly appreciated. However, having been born into it perhaps we sometimes took it for granted. The Buddha himself said, "Test my words as carefully as goldsmiths assay gold and only then accept them." The Buddha taught people of all backgrounds and levels of intelligence for a long period of time. Consequently, each of his teachings must be weighed carefully for meaning and evaluated to determine whether it is literally true or only figuratively so. Many teachings were given in particular circumstances or to beings of limited understanding. Accepting any doctrine or aspect of a doctrine without first scrutinizing it analytically is like building a castle upon ice—one's practice will be unstable and lack fundamental strength and depth.

PRACTICING DHARMA

What does "practice Dharma" mean? Literally translated, Dharma means "that which holds"; it is the spiritual teaching that keeps or leads us out of suffering. Buddhism asserts that although at the moment our mind is overpowered by delusion and distortion, ultimately there is an aspect of mind that is by nature pure and unstained, and that by cultivating this purity and eliminating mental obscurations we are "held back" from suffering and unsatisfying experiences.

Buddha taught the potential purity of mind as a fundamental tenet of his doctrine, and Dharmakirti, the Indian logician who appeared a millennium later, established its validity logically. When this seed of enlightenment has been sufficiently cultivated, we gain the experience of nirvana, freedom from all the shortcomings of samsara. As well as the concept of the seed of enlightenment, Dharmakirti validated logically the entire spectrum of Buddhist tenets, including the law of karma, the concept of rebirth, the possibility of liberation and omniscience, and the nature of the Three Jewels of Refuge: Buddha, Dharma and Sangha.

As for the actual mode of practice, it's a mistake to practice without a logical understanding of the doctrine. We should know well just what we are doing and why, especially those of us who are monks or nuns and have dedicated our entire lives to the practice of Dharma; we should be particularly careful to practice immaculately. The Sangha is very important to the stability of the doctrine; therefore, we should do our best to emulate the Buddha himself. Those considering ordination should first think well; there is no need to become a monk just to be an inferior monk. The Sangha has the responsibility of embodying the precepts. If you want to lead an ordinary life, leave monasticism to those of greater spiritual inclination and simply practice as a layperson as best you can.

All world religions are similar in that they provide methods for cultivating wholesome aspects of mind and eliminating unwholesome ones. Buddhism is a particularly rich religion because, having developed in India when the country was at a high point spiritually and philosophically, it presents both a total range of spiritual ideas and a rational approach to the methods of spiritual development. This is particularly important in this modern era, when the rational mind is given such credence.

Because of this aspect of rationality, Buddhism finds little difficulty in confronting the modern world. Indeed, many of the findings of modern science, such as those of nuclear physics, which are considered new discoveries, have long been discussed in ancient Buddhist scriptures. Because the Buddha's last advice to his disciples was that they should never accept anything on faith alone but only through rational investigation, the Buddhist world has always managed to keep the spirit of inquiry very much alive within its precincts. This is unlike many other religions, which lay claims on the truth and thus never allow any type of investigation that seems to threaten their limited descriptions of reality.

THE THREE JEWELS OF REFUGE

Whether or not you are a Buddhist is determined by whether or not you have taken refuge in the Three Jewels—Buddha, Dharma and Sangha—purely, from the depths of your heart. Simply reciting Buddhist prayers, playing with a rosary or walking around temples does not make you a Buddhist. Even a monkey can be taught to do these things. Dharma is a matter of mind and spirit, not external activities. Therefore, to be a Buddhist, you must understand exactly what the Three Jewels of Refuge are and how they relate to your spiritual life.

With respect to refuge in the Buddha, we talk about the *causal* Buddha refuge—all the buddhas of the past, present and future, of whom the most relevant to us is Buddha Shakyamuni—and the *resultant* Buddha refuge—refuge in our own potentiality for enlightenment, the buddha that each of us will become. As for refuge in the

Dharma, there is the Dharma that was taught in the scriptures and that which is the spiritual realization of what was taught. Finally, we take refuge in the Sangha, in both ordinary monks and nuns, who are symbols of the Sangha, and the *arya* Sangha—those beings who have gained meditational experience of the ultimate mode of truth. Therefore, we say that the Buddha is the teacher, Dharma is the way and Sangha are the helpful spiritual companions.

Of these three, the most important to us as individuals is the Dharma, for ultimately only we can help ourselves—nobody else can achieve our enlightenment for us or give it to us. Enlightenment comes only to the person who practices Dharma well, who takes the Dharma and applies it to the cultivation of his or her own mental continuum. Therefore, of the Three Jewels, the Dharma is the ultimate refuge. By hearing, contemplating and meditating on the Dharma our lives can become one with it and enlightenment an immediate possibility.

KARMA

All the great Kadampa masters of the past stressed that refuge must be practiced in the context of an intense awareness of the law of cause and effect; it requires observance of the law of karma as its support. The Buddha said, "You are your own protector and your own enemy." The Buddha cannot protect us; only our own observance of the law of karma can. If we keep our refuge purely and live in accordance with karma, we become our own protector; if we don't, if we live in a way contradictory to the spiritual path and become our own worst enemy, we harm ourselves in this and future lives.

The mind of an ordinary person is undisciplined and uncontrolled. To be able to engage in higher Buddhist practices, such as the development of single-pointed concentration, insight into emptiness or the yogic methods of the various tantric systems, we must first cultivate a disciplined mind. On the basis of refuge and self-discipline we can easily develop ever-increasing experiences in higher Dharma practices, but without the foundation of discipline our higher practices will yield no fruit.

DEVELOPING PRACTICE

We all want to practice the highest techniques but first we have to ask ourselves if we have mastered the lower prerequisites, such as discipline. The aim of refuge is to transform an ordinary person into a buddha, and when this has been accomplished the purpose of refuge has been fulfilled. The moment our mind becomes Buddha, our speech becomes Dharma and our body, Sangha. However, the attainment of this exalted state depends upon our own practice of Dharma. Leaving practice to others while hoping for spiritual benefits for ourselves is an impossible dream.

In order to purify our mind of karmic and perception-related mistakes and cultivate the qualities of enlightenment within our stream of being, we ourselves must perform the practices and experience the spiritual states. The 108 volumes of the Buddha's word that were translated into Tibetan have one essential theme: purify the mind and generate inner qualities. Nowhere does it say that somebody else can do this for us. Therefore, in a way, the buddhas are somewhat limited—they can liberate us only by means of inspiring us to practice their teachings. Many buddhas have come before but we are still here in samsara. This is not because those buddhas lacked compassion for us but because we were unable to practice their teachings. Individuals' progress along the spiritual path depends upon the efforts of those individuals themselves.

THE TEN VIRTUOUS ACTIONS

The process of self-cultivation has many levels. For beginners, however, the first necessity is to avoid the ten nonvirtuous actions and observe their opposites, the ten virtuous actions. Three of these ten actions are physical: instead of killing we should value and cherish life; instead of stealing we should give freely of what we can to help others; and instead of taking others' partners we should respect their feelings. Four actions concern speech: instead of lying we should speak the truth; instead of causing disharmony by slandering others we should encourage virtue by speaking about their good qualities; instead of speaking harshly and sharply our words should be soft, gentle and loving; and instead of conversing meaninglessly we should engage in meaningful activities. Finally, three of the ten actions concern mind: we should replace attachment with non-attachment; ill will toward others with feelings of love and compassion; and incorrect beliefs with realistic attitudes.

Every Buddhist should follow these ten fundamental disciplines. Not doing so while engaging in so-called higher tantric methods is simply fooling yourself. These ten are simple practices, observances that anybody can follow, yet they are the first step for anybody wanting to work toward the powerful yogas that bring enlightenment in one lifetime.

When we take refuge and become a Buddhist we must honor the family of buddhas. Engaging in any of the ten nonvirtues after having taken refuge is to disgrace Buddhism. Nobody is asking you to be a Buddhist; you're a Buddhist because you've chosen to be. Therefore you should qualify yourself accordingly, and the minimal qualification is to avoid the ten nonvirtues and cultivate their opposites. Granted, nobody is perfect, but if you want to call yourself a Buddhist, you have to exert some effort. When something causes attachment or anger to arise within you, the least you should do is make an effort not to be overcome by that distorted state of mind and instead maintain a free and loving attitude.

CULTIVATING THE MIND

The essence of Dharma is cultivation of the mind because all the positive and negative karmas of body and speech originate in and are given direction by the mind. If you do not cultivate an awareness of your mental processes and the ability to cut off negative streams of thought as they arise, twenty years of meditation in a remote cave will be of little value. Before looking for a cave you should look for good qualities in your mind and develop the ability to live in accordance with Dharma. Only then will sitting in a cave be better than a bear's hibernation. Talking about doing tantric retreat while the ten foundations of Dharma are still beyond you is simply making yourself a laughing stock.

MAKING THIS LIFE USEFUL

As humans, we have the potential to attain enlightenment in a single lifetime. However, life is short and much of it has already passed by. We should ask ourselves how much spiritual progress we have made. Death can arrive at any moment and when it does we must leave behind everything except the mental imprints of our life's deeds. If we have practiced and tried to live in accordance with Dharma during our life, or even gained realizations, that energy will be there within our mind. On the other hand, if we have spent our life in nonvirtue, negative thoughts and memories of our samsaric ways will occupy our consciousness when it goes to the next life.

Therefore, now, while we have the ability, we should practice Dharma intensively and purely. Dharma practice will bring peace and harmony to both ourselves and those around us, even in this life, and, should we not achieve enlightenment in this lifetime, it will give us a wish-fulfilling jewel that we can carry into future lives to help us continue along on the spiritual path.

Ultimately, our future is in our own hands. Most people make fantastic plans for next week, next month and next year, but what counts most is to practice Dharma right now. If we do this, all our aims will be fulfilled. When we cultivate virtuous activities today, the laws of dependent arising ensure that a positive stream of change is set in motion. This is the preciousness of being human: we are able to affect dynamically our own future state of being by applying discriminating wisdom to all the actions of our body, speech and mind. To use and cultivate this discriminating wisdom is to extract the very essence of the human life.

───────────■───────────

His Holiness the Dalai Lama (1935–) is the spiritual leader of Tibet and was head of state until 2011. Forced into exile in 1959 by the illegal Chinese communist colonization of Tibet, which continues to this day, he has continued to inspire the Tibetan people and also inspires millions of others the world over. In 1989 he received the Nobel Peace Prize for his efforts to find a non-violent solution to China's brutal occupation of his country. He gave this teaching in Delhi in the early 1960s. It was translated by Losang Chöpel and Glenn H. Mullin and first published in English in 1981 in *Teachings at Tushita*.

GENERATING BODHICITTA

His Holiness Ling Rinpoche

Bodhicitta and Wisdom

T HE ENLIGHTENED ATTITUDE, bodhicitta, which has love and compassion as its basis, is the essential seed producing the attainment of buddhahood. Therefore, it is a subject that should be approached with the pure thought, "May I gain enlightenment in order to be of greatest benefit to the world."

If we want to attain the state of the full enlightenment of buddhahood as opposed to the lesser enlightenment of an *arhat*—nirvana, or individual liberation—our innermost practice must be the cultivation of bodhicitta. If meditation on emptiness is our innermost practice, we run the risk of falling into nirvana instead of gaining buddhahood. This teaching is given in the saying, "When the father is bodhicitta and the mother is wisdom, the child joins the caste of the buddhas." In ancient India, children of inter-caste marriages would adopt the caste of the father, regardless of the caste of the mother. Therefore, bodhicitta is like the father: if we cultivate bodhicitta, we enter the caste of the buddhas.

Although bodhicitta is the principal cause of buddhahood, bodhicitta as the father must unite with wisdom, or meditation on emptiness, as the mother in order to produce a child capable of attaining buddhahood. One without the other does not bring full enlightenment. Even though bodhicitta is the essential energy that produces buddhahood, throughout the stages of its development it should be combined with meditation on emptiness. In the *Perfection of Wisdom Sutras,* where the Buddha spoke most extensively on emptiness, we are constantly reminded to practice our meditation on emptiness within the context of bodhicitta.

However, the spiritual effects of receiving teachings on bodhicitta are quite limited if we lack a certain spiritual foundation. Consequently most teachers insist that we first cultivate various preliminary practices within ourselves before approaching this higher precept. If we want to go to university, we must first learn to read and write. Of course, while merely hearing about meditation on love, compassion and bodhicitta does leave a favorable imprint on our mental continuum, for the teaching to really produce a definite inner transformation, we first have to meditate extensively on preliminaries such as the perfect human rebirth, impermanence and death, the nature of karma and samsara, refuge and the higher trainings in ethics, meditation and wisdom.

What precisely is bodhicitta? It is the mind strongly characterized by the aspiration, "For the sake of all sentient beings I must attain the state of full enlightenment." While it's easy to repeat these words to ourselves, bodhicitta is much deeper than that. It is a quality we cultivate systematically within our mind. Merely holding the thought "I must attain enlightenment for the sake of benefiting others" in mind without first cultivating its prerequisite causes, stages and basic foundations will not give birth to bodhicitta. For this reason, the venerable Atisha once asked, "Do you know anybody with bodhicitta not born from meditation on love and compassion?"

THE BENEFITS OF BODHICITTA

What are the benefits of generating bodhicitta? If we know the qualities of good food, we'll attempt to obtain, prepare and eat it. Similarly, when we hear of the great qualities of bodhicitta we'll seek to learn the methods and practices for generating it.

The immediate benefit of generating bodhicitta within our mindstream is that we enter the great vehicle leading to buddhahood and gain the title of bodhisattva, a child of the buddhas. It does not matter what we look like, how we dress, how wealthy or powerful we are, whether or not we have clairvoyance or miraculous powers, or how learned we are, as soon as we generate bodhicitta we become bodhisattvas; regardless of our other qualities, if we do not have bodhicitta we are not bodhisattvas. Even a being with bodhicitta who [intentionally] takes rebirth in an animal body is respected by all the buddhas as a bodhisattva.

The great sages of the lesser vehicle possess numberless wonderful qualities but in terms of nature, a person who has developed even the initial stages of bodhicitta surpasses them. This is similar to the way that the baby son of a universal monarch who, although only an infant possessing no qualities of knowledge or power, is accorded higher status than any scholar or minister in the realm.

In terms of conventional benefit, all the happiness and goodness that exists comes from bodhicitta. Buddhas are born from bodhisattvas but bodhisattvas come from bodhicitta. As a result of the birth of buddhas and bodhisattvas, great waves of enlightened energy spread throughout the universe, influencing sentient beings to create positive karma. This positive karma in turn brings them much benefit and happiness. On the one hand, the mighty stream of enlightened and enlightening energy issues from the wisdom body of the buddhas, but since the buddhas are born from bodhisattvas and bodhisattvas from bodhicitta, the ultimate source of universal goodness and happiness is bodhicitta itself.

How to develop bodhicitta

How do we develop bodhicitta? There are two major methods. The first of these, the six causes and one effect, applies six causal meditations—recognizing that all sentient beings were once our own mother, a mother's kindness, repaying such kindness, love, compassion and the extraordinary thought of universal responsibility—to produce one result: bodhicitta. The second technique is the meditation in which we directly change self-cherishing into the cherishing of others.

In order to practice either of these methods of developing bodhicitta we must first develop a sense of equanimity toward all living beings.[16] We must transcend seeing some beings as close friends,

---

[16] See Lama Zopa Rinpoche's equilibrium meditation, appendix 1.

others as disliked or hated enemies and the rest as merely unknown strangers. Until we have developed equanimity for all beings, any meditation we do in an attempt to develop bodhicitta will not be effective. For example, if we want to paint a mural on a wall we must first get rid of all the cracks and lumps on its surface. Similarly, we cannot create the beautiful bodhicitta within our mind until it has been purified of the distortions of seeing others as friend, enemy or stranger.

THE ATTITUDE OF DISCRIMINATION

The way we impute this discrimination upon others is quite automatic and, as a result, whenever we see somebody we have labeled "friend," attachment arises and we respond with warmth and kindness. Why have we labeled this person "friend"? It is only because on some level or other this person has benefited or supported us. Alternatively, whenever we encounter somebody we have labeled "enemy," aversion arises and we respond with coldness and anger. The reason is again because that person once harmed or threatened us in some way. Similarly, when we encounter somebody who has neither helped nor harmed us, we apply the label "stranger" and have no feelings for that person one way or the other.

However, if we examine this method of discriminating others we will quickly see that it is an extremely unstable process. Even in this life, people once regarded as friends become enemies and enemies often become friends. And in the countless lives we have taken since beginningless time while spinning on the wheel of life, there is not one sentient being who has consistently been either friend or enemy.

Our best friend of this life could easily have been our worst enemy in a previous incarnation and *vice versa*. A friend who mistreats us quickly becomes an enemy and an enemy who helps us soon becomes a new-found friend. So which one is really the friend and which one the enemy? Instead of responding to others on the basis of the ephemeral benefit or harm they bring us we should meditate that all have alternately benefited and harmed us in the stream of our infinite past lives and, in that way, abandon superficial discriminations.

A root cause of this discriminating mind is the self-cherishing attitude, the thought that makes us consider ourselves more important than others. As a result of self-cherishing we develop attachment to those who help us and aversion to those who cause us problems. This, in turn, causes us to create countless negative karmas trying to support the "helpers" and overcome the "harmers." Thus, as the karmic seeds of these actions ripen into suffering experiences, we bring great misery upon others and ourselves, both now and in future lives.

THE BENEFITS OF CHERISHING OTHERS

A teaching says, "All happiness in the world arises from cherishing others; every suffering arises from self-cherishing." Why is this so? From self-cherishing comes the wish to further oneself even at others' expense. This causes all the killing, stealing, intolerance and so forth that we see everywhere around us. As well as destroying the happiness of this life, these negative activities plant karmic seeds for a future rebirth in the miserable realms of existence—the hell, hungry ghost and animal realms. Self-cherishing is responsible for every conflict, from family problems to international wars and for all the negative karma thus created.

What are the results of cherishing others? If we cherish others, we won't harm or kill them—this is conducive to our own long life. When we cherish others, we're open to and empathetic with them and live in generosity—this is a karmic cause of our own future prosperity. If we cherish others, even when somebody harms or makes problems for us, we are able to abide in love and patience—a karmic cause of a beautiful form in future lives. In short, every auspicious condition arises from the positive karma generated by cherishing others. These conditions themselves bring joy and happiness and, in addition, act as causes for the attainment of liberation and buddhahood.

How? To attain liberation we have to master the three higher trainings in moral discipline, meditation and wisdom. Of these, the first is the most important because it is the basis for the development of the other two. The essence of moral discipline is abandoning any action that harms others. If we cherish others more than ourselves, we will not find this discipline difficult. Our mind will be calm and peaceful, which is conducive to both meditation and wisdom.

Looking at it another way, cherishing others is the proper and noble approach to take. In this life, everything that comes to us is directly or indirectly due to the kindness of others. We buy food from others in the market; the clothing we wear and the houses we live in depend upon the help of others. And to attain the ultimate goals of nirvana and buddhahood, we are completely dependent upon others; without them we would be unable to meditate upon love, compassion, trust and so forth and thus could not generate spiritual experiences.

Also, any meditation teaching we receive has come from the Buddha through the kindness of sentient beings. The Buddha taught only to benefit sentient beings; if there were no sentient beings he would not have taught. Therefore, in his *Guide to the Bodhisattva's Way of Life*, Shantideva comments that in terms of kindness, sentient beings are equal to the buddhas. Sometimes people have respect and devotion for the buddhas but dislike sentient beings. That is mistaken. We should appreciate sentient beings just as much as we do the buddhas themselves.

If we look at happiness and harmony, we will find their cause to be universal caring. The cause of unhappiness and disharmony is self-cherishing.

At one time the Buddha was an ordinary person like us. Then he abandoned self-cherishing and replaced it with universal caring and entered the path to buddhahood. Because we still cling to the self-cherishing mind, we are left behind in samsara, benefiting neither ourselves nor others.

One of the *Jataka Tales*—accounts of the Buddha's previous lives—tells the story of an incarnation in which the Buddha was a huge turtle that took pity on some shipwreck victims and carried them to shore on its back. Once ashore, the exhausted turtle fell into a faint, but as he slept he was attacked by thousands of ants. Soon the biting of the ants woke the turtle up, but he saw that if he were to move, he would kill innumerable creatures. Therefore, he remained still and offered his body to the insects as food. This shows how much the Buddha cherished living beings. Many of the *Jataka Tales* tell similar stories of the Buddha's previous lives in which he showed the importance of cherishing others. *The Wish-Fulfilling Tree* contains 108 such stories.

Essentially, self-cherishing is the cause of every undesirable experience and universal caring is the cause of every happiness. The sufferings of both the lower and upper realms of existence, all interferences to spiritual practice, and even the subtle limitations of liberation come from self-cherishing, while every happiness of this and future lives comes from cherishing others.

ENGAGING IN BODHICITTA

Therefore, we should contemplate deeply the benefits of cherishing others and try to develop an open, loving attitude toward all living beings. This should not be an inert emotion but one characterized by great compassion—the wish to separate others from their suffering. Whenever we encounter a being in suffering we should react like a mother seeing her only child caught in a fire or fallen into a terrible river. Our main thought should be to help others. With respect to those in states of suffering, we should think, "May I help separate them from their suffering"; with respect to those in states of happiness, we should think, "May I help them maintain their happiness." We should direct this attitude equally toward all beings.

Some people feel strong compassion for friends or relatives in trouble but none for unpleasant people or enemies. This is not spiritual compassion; it is merely a form of attachment. True compassion does not discriminate between beings; it regards all equally.

Similarly, true love is the desire to maintain the happiness of all beings impartially, regardless of whether we like them or not. Spiritual love is of two main types: that merely possessing equanimity and that possessing the active wish to maintain others' happiness. When we meditate repeatedly on how all beings have in previous lives been mother, father and friend to us, we soon come to have equanimity toward them all. Eventually this develops into an overwhelming wish to see all beings possess happiness and the causes of happiness. This is great, undiscriminating love.

By meditating properly on love and compassion, we produce what are called the eight great benefits. These condense into two: happiness in this and future lives for both ourselves and others and development along the path to full and perfect buddhahood. Such meditation results in rebirth in the three upper realms as a human or a god and fertilizes the seeds of enlightenment.

In brief, we should have the wish to help others maintain their happiness and separate them from suffering regardless of whether they have acted as friend or enemy to us. Moreover, we should develop a personal sense of responsibility for their happiness. This is called the "special" or "higher" thought and is marked by a strong sense of responsibility for the welfare of others. It is like taking the responsibility of going to the market to get somebody exactly what she needs instead of just sitting reflecting on how nice it would be if she had what she wanted. We take upon ourselves the responsibility of actually fulfilling others' requirements.

Then we should ask ourselves, "Do I have the ability to benefit all others?" Obviously we do not. Who has such ability? Only an enlightened being, a buddha, has the ability to fully and completely benefit others. Why? Because only those who have attained buddhahood are fully developed and completely separated from limitations;

those still in samsara cannot place others in nirvana. Even *shravaka* arhats or tenth-level bodhisattvas are unable to benefit others fully because they themselves still have limitations, but buddhas spontaneously and automatically benefit all beings with every breath they take. The enlightened state is metaphorically likened to the drum of Brahma, which automatically booms teachings to the world, or to a cloud, which spontaneously gives cooling shade and life-giving water wherever it goes.

To fulfill others' needs, we should seek to place them in the total peace and maturity of buddhahood; to be able to do this, we must first gain buddhahood ourselves. The state of buddhahood is an evolutionary result of bodhicitta. Bodhicitta is born from the special thought of universal responsibility—the thought of benefiting all others by oneself alone. To drink water we must have both the desire to drink and a container for the water. The wish to benefit others by placing them in buddhahood is like the desire to drink and the wish to attain enlightenment oneself in order to benefit them in this way is like the container. When both are present, we can benefit others and ourselves.

If we hear about the meditations that generate bodhicitta and try to practice them without first refining our mind with the preliminary meditations, it is very unlikely that we'll make much inner progress. For example, if we meditate on compassion without first gaining some experience of the meditations on the four noble truths, or at least on the truth of suffering, we'll develop merely a superficial understanding. How can we experience mature compassion, the aspiration to free all beings from suffering, when we do not know the deeper levels of suffering that permeate the human psyche? How can we relate to others' suffering when we do not even know the subtle levels of frustration and tension pervading our own being? In order to know the workings of our own mind, we have to know every aspect of suffering; only then can we be in a position to empathize with the hearts and minds of others. We must have compassion for ourselves before we can have it for others.

Through meditation on suffering, we can generate a certain level of renunciation, or spiritual stability. This stability should be guarded and cultivated by the various methods taught on the small and intermediate stages of training, which are the two main steps in approaching the meditations on bodhicitta. As we progress in our meditations on the suffering nature of life and the causes of this suffering, we begin to search for the path leading to transcendence of imperfection. We meditate upon the precious nature and unique opportunities of human existence, which makes us appreciate our situation. We then meditate upon impermanence and death, which helps us transcend grasping at the petty aspects of life and directs our mind to search for spiritual knowledge.

Because spiritual knowledge is not gained from books or without cause, its cause must be cultivated. This means training properly under a fully qualified spiritual master and generating the practices as instructed.

Nevertheless, merely hearing about bodhicitta is very beneficial because it provides a seed for the development of the enlightened spirit. However, cultivation of this seed to fruition requires careful practice. We must progress through the actual inner experiences of the above-mentioned meditations, and for this we require close contact with a meditation teacher able to supervise and guide our evolution. In order for our teacher's presence to be of maximum benefit, we should learn the correct attitudes and actions for cultivating an effective guru-disciple relationship. Then, step-by-step, the seeds of bodhicitta our teacher plants within us can grow to full maturity and unfold the lotus of enlightenment within us.

This is only a brief description of bodhicitta and the methods of developing it. If it inspires an interest in this topic within you, I'll be very happy. The basis of bodhicitta—love and compassion—is a force that brings every benefit to both yourself and others, and if this can be transformed into bodhicitta itself, your every action will become a cause of omniscient buddhahood. Even if you can practice to the point of simply slightly weakening your self-cherishing attitude, I'll be very grateful. Without first generating bodhicitta, buddhahood is completely out of the question; once bodhicitta has started to grow, perfect enlightenment is only a matter of time.

You should try to meditate regularly on death and impermanence and thus become a spiritual practitioner of small scope. Then you should develop the meditations on the unsatisfactory nature of samsara and the three higher trainings of ethics, concentration and wisdom and thus become a practitioner of medium scope. Finally, you should give birth to love, compassion, universal responsibility and bodhicitta and thus enter the path of the practitioner of great scope, the Mahayana, which has full buddhahood as its goal. Relying on the guidance of a spiritual master, you should cultivate the seeds of bodhicitta in connection with the wisdom of emptiness and, for the sake of all that lives, quickly actualize buddhahood. This may not be an easy task, but it has ultimate perfection as its fruit.

The most important step in spiritual growth is the first: the decision to avoid evil and cultivate goodness within your stream of being. On the basis of this fundamental discipline, every spiritual quality becomes possible, even the eventual perfection of buddhahood.

Each of us has the potential to do this; each of us can become a perfect being. All we have to do is direct our energy toward learning and then enthusiastically practice the teachings. As bodhicitta is the very essence of all the Buddha's teachings, we should make every effort to realize it.

Kyabje Ling Rinpoche (1903–83), the late senior tutor to His Holiness the Dalai Lama, was the 97th holder of the Throne of Ganden and thus head of the Gelug tradition of Tibetan Buddhism. He gave this teaching at Tushita Mahayana Meditation Centre, 14 November 1979. It was translated by Gelek Rimpoche and first published in *Teachings at Tushita* in 1981.

CREATING SPACE FOR DHARMA

Lama Yeshe

MAKING DHARMA PRACTICE EFFECTIVE

THE ANTIDOTE TO delusion, ego and every other problem we face is the wisdom of Dharma; Dharma wisdom provides the deepest solution to every human problem. Whoever has problems needs Dharma; Dharma wisdom is the light that eliminates the dark shadow of ignorance, the main source of all human afflictions.

Dharma philosophy is not Dharma; doctrine is not Dharma; religious art is not Dharma. Dharma is not the statue of Lord Buddha on your altar. Dharma is the inner understanding of reality that leads us beyond the dark shadow of ignorance, beyond dissatisfaction.

It is not enough merely to accept Dharma as being true. We must also understand our individual reality, our specific needs and the purpose of Dharma as it relates to us as individuals. If we accept Dharma for reasons of custom or culture alone, it does not become properly effective for our mind. For example, it's wrong for me to think, "I'm Tibetan, therefore, I'm a Mahayanist." Perhaps I can talk about Mahayana philosophy, but *being* a Mahayanist, having Mahayana Dharma in my heart, is something else.

You may have been born in a Dharma country, in an environment where religion is accepted, but if you do not use that religion to gain an understanding of the reality of your own mind, there is little sense in being a believer. Dharma cannot solve your problems if you do not approach it pragmatically. You should seek Dharma knowledge in order to stop your problems, to make yourself spiritually healthy—in religious terms, to discover eternal happiness, peace and bliss.

We ourselves are responsible for discovering our own peace and liberation. We cannot say that some other power, like God, is responsible—if we do, we are weak and not taking responsibility for the actions of our own body, speech and mind. Buddhists understand that they are personally responsible for everything they do: it's in their own hands whether their actions are positive or negative. Therefore, although we might find ourselves in a religious environment—in India, Tibet or even the West—*becoming* religious is something else.

External cultural aspects do not indicate the presence of Dharma. Dharma is that which leads us beyond delusion, beyond ego, beyond the usual human problems. If we use it for such purposes we can say, "I'm practicing Dharma," but if we don't, there's little benefit in reciting even the most powerful mantras.

One of the most fundamental Buddhist teachings is to renounce samsara. That doesn't mean we shouldn't drink water when we're thirsty. It means that we must understand samsara such that even when we're caught in a samsaric situation, no karmic reaction ensues. The application of skillful method and wisdom is the real renunciation; as long as we have grasping and hatred in our mind, we have not renounced samsara.

We can change our clothes and shave our head, but when we ask yourselves, "What have I really renounced?" we may find that our mind is exactly the same as it was before our external transformation—we have not stopped our problems.

That's why we call samsara a cycle; cyclic existence. We do things—we change, change, change, change—we enjoy the novelty of every change, but actually, all we're doing is creating more karma. Every time we do something, there's a reaction that makes our bondage in cyclic existence even tighter than it was before. That's samsara. To loosen this tightness we need the wisdom that illuminates the darkness of ignorance. It's not enough to think, "I am Buddhist; Buddha will take care of me"; "I am Christian; God will take care of me." Belief is not enough; we have to understand the reality of our own mind.

To this end, Lord Buddha taught many meditation techniques to wake us up from ignorance. First we have to understand our needs as individuals; according to Lord Buddha's teachings each of us has different needs. Usually we ignore these and, without discriminating wisdom, just accept whatever comes along. As a result, we end up in a situation from which we cannot escape. That is samsara.

UNDERSTANDING OURSELVES

Moreover, it is important for us to recognize that even if right now some of our habits and attitudes are wrong, it's possible to change and transform them. Grasping at permanence makes us think that we're unchanging. This negative thought pattern is very strong and prevents us from developing or acting in a Dharma way. To help us overcome our wrong conceptions, Lord Buddha taught the four noble truths.[17] As the first characteristic of the noble truth of suffering, he taught impermanence.

It is very important to understand impermanence. When we understand the impermanent nature of things, their non-stop change, we give ourselves the time and space to accept whatever situation comes along. Then, even if we are in a suffering situation, we can take care of ourselves; we can look at it without getting upset. Otherwise, our upset or guilty mind prevents us from waking from confusion, from seeing our own clarity.

Clarity always exists within us. The nature of our consciousness is clear. It is merely a question of seeing it. If you always feel dirty, negative and hopeless, as if you're somebody who could never possibly discover inner peace and liberation, you're reacting to a deluded, negative mind, a fixed conception. You're thinking beyond reality, beyond the nature of phenomena; you're not in touch with reality. You have to eradicate such preconceived ideas before you can cultivate tranquility and peace, before your intelligence can touch reality.

Check up right now. Ask yourself, "What am I?" "Who am I?" Even on the conventional plane, when you ask yourself this you

---

[17] See the Dalai Lama's teaching on the four noble truths, p. 97

find that you're holding a permanent conception of your self of yesterday, the day before yesterday, last week, last month, last year.... This idea of the self is not correct. It's a preconception that must be broken down and recognized as unreasonable. Then you can understand the possibility of ceaseless, infinite development and spiritual growth.

The beauty of being human is that we can continuously develop inner qualities such as peace, the energy of the enlightenment experience and bliss and eventually transcend our dualistic mind. When we come to understand this inner beauty, we stop grasping at external objects, which can never bring eternal satisfaction. This is an important sign of spiritual progress. We cannot simultaneously be religious and grasp at material things; the two are incompatible.

We see people getting more and more confused and dissatisfied the more possessions they get until finally they commit suicide. Sometimes the poor don't understand this; they think that materially wealthy people must be happy. They are not happy. They are dissatisfied, emotionally disturbed, confused and immersed in suffering. Suicide rates are much higher in affluent societies than in economically undeveloped ones. This is not Dharma philosophy—this is present-day reality, our twentieth century situation; it's happening right now. I am not suggesting that you give up your material comfort; Lord Buddha never said that we have to give up our enjoyments. Rather, he taught that we should avoid confusing ourselves by grasping at worldly pleasures.

The underlying attitude that forces us to chase after unworthy objects is the delusion that causes us to think, "This object will give me satisfaction; without it life would be hopeless." These preconceptions make us incapable of dealing with the new situations that inevitably arise from day to day. We expect things to happen in a certain way and when they don't, we can't cope with them properly. Instead of handling unexpected situations effectively we become tense, frustrated and psychologically disturbed.

DEVELOPING OUR DHARMA EXPERIENCE

Most of us are emotionally unstable: sometimes up, sometimes down. When life is going well we put on a very religious aspect but when things go badly we lose it completely. This shows that we have no inner conviction, that our understanding of Dharma is very limited and fickle.

People say, "I've been practicing Dharma for years but I've still got all these problems. I don't think Buddhism helps." My question to them is, "Have you developed single-pointed concentration or penetrative insight?" That's the problem. Simply saying, "Oh yes, I understand. I pray every day; I'm a good person" is not enough. Dharma is a total way of life. It's not just for breakfast, Sundays, or the temple. If you're subdued and controlled in the temple but aggressive and uncontrolled outside of it, your understanding of Dharma is neither continuous nor indestructible.

Are you satisfied with your present state of mind? Probably not, and that's why you need meditation, why you need Dharma. Worldly possessions do not give you satisfaction; you can't depend on transitory objects for your happiness.

When we refugees fled Tibet we left behind our beautiful environment and way of life. If my mind had been fixed in its belief that my happiness and pleasure depended solely upon being in the country of my birth, I could never have been happy in India. I would have thought, "There are no snow mountains here; I can't be happy." Mental attitude is the main problem; physical problems are secondary. Therefore, avoid grasping at material objects and seek instead an indestructible understanding of the ultimate nature of the mind.

DEVELOPING CONCENTRATION AND INSIGHT

Dharma practice does not depend on cultural conditions. Whether we travel by train, plane or automobile we can still practice Dharma. However, in order to completely destroy the root of the dualistic mind, a partial understanding of the reality of our own mind is not sufficient. Dharma practice requires continual, sustained effort; just a few flashes of understanding are not enough. To fully penetrate to the ultimate reality of our own mind, we have to develop single-pointed concentration. When we have done so, our understanding will be continuous and indestructible.

Lord Buddha's teachings on single-pointed concentration are very important because they show us how to transcend worldly conceptions. However, single-pointed concentration alone is not enough. We have to combine it with penetrative insight. What's the difference between the two? First we develop single-pointed concentration, which leads us beyond worldly emotional problems and gives us a degree of higher satisfaction. But a certain amount of darkness remains in our mind. In order to reach the depths of human consciousness we also have to cultivate penetrative insight, which is the only thing that can lead us totally beyond the dualistic view of all existence. From the Buddhist point of view, the dualistic way of thinking is the real conflict. Meditative concentration can bring us a certain degree of peace, but if the dualistic view remains, we still have conflict in our mind.

The purpose of insight meditation, the experience of emptiness, is realization of non-duality, where the flashing of sense objects and images disappears and we experience the total unity of ultimate reality. There's a difference between the *experience* of emptiness and its philosophy. Philosophically speaking, sense objects exist, sense pleasures exist, and there's a relationship between the senses and the external world. But in the experience itself, there is no awareness of a duality, no perception of the sense world, and no sense of conflict to irritate the mind. Normally, whenever we perceive objects in the sense world, we see two things: we perceive the thing itself and immediately compare it with something else. Society is built on the dualistic mind. Eventually it comes down to, if my next-door neighbor gets a car I'm going to want one, too. Two forces are at work, and one becomes the reason for the other.

From the Buddhist point of view, any information received through the five sense consciousnesses is always distorted by dualistic grasping. It's like an optical illusion. It registers in our consciousness and we believe that what we're seeing is true. Actually, it's an unreal distortion and it gives birth to every other delusion.

Consequently, the Buddhist attitude toward data received through the five sense consciousnesses is one of mistrust. You cannot rely on the judgments of good and bad that come through your senses— they always give you a dualistic, distorted impression. You'd be better off going around with your eyes closed!

Anyway, always question and be critical of the information that comes in through your senses. That's the way to eventually transcend ordinariness, karmically-created actions and the inevitable reactions of dissatisfaction.

Q. Are you saying that we are able to fully realize emptiness?
Lama. Definitely! How? By examining the nature of your own mind, repeatedly asking yourself, "What am I?" "Who am I?" Eventually, you'll come to see the falsity of your instinctive ego-model and how it projects itself into your life, causing you to misinterpret every experience you have. When you discover this wrong view, you're close to understanding emptiness. Until you discover how ego-grasping works within you, realization of emptiness is a long way off.

Q. What is the relationship between emptiness and consciousness?
Lama. Consciousness is not emptiness. But when you understand the nature of consciousness, the clarity of mind, you have an experience very similar to that of the perception of emptiness. Therefore, in the Tibetan tradition of Mahayana Buddhism, we emphasize contemplating your own consciousness as a preliminary leading to the experience of ultimate emptiness.

Q. You spoke of sensory awareness disappearing in the experience of emptiness. How can we perceive the world without the five sense consciousnesses?

Lama. Well, there are both ultimate and conventional worlds. In the beginning, you meditate on the nature of the conventional world and this then becomes the method by which the ultimate is discovered. Look at the sense world but don't be entranced by it. Be constantly analytical, always checking to see that your perception is clear and free from ego-based exaggeration. Conventional reality is not the problem; the problem is that in your perception of things, you exaggerate and distort the various aspects of an object. Therefore, you must continually question your experience. You can't simply say, "It's right because I saw it and wrong because I didn't." You have to go deeper than that.

Q. When you put a question to your mind, to whom do you put the question?

Lama. When you question your own consciousness, you question your wrong conceptions, your belief in nonexistent entities. When you see a red glass, you recognize it as a red glass, but inside you raise doubts: "Maybe it's red, maybe it's white." Whenever you question, answers come. Usually we just accept whatever happens without question. As a result, we're deluded and polluted. To question is to seek, and the answer lies within you. We feel that our consciousness is small, but it is like a mighty ocean in which everything can be found. When I talk, you may think, "Maybe this lama will give me some realization," but there is no realization to give. To talk about Dharma is to throw switches here and there, hoping to wake people up. Belief in the Buddha, Krishna or whomever is not enough; you must take responsibility for your own body, speech and mind. We all have a certain degree of wisdom; this must be cultivated. All religions use bells, Buddhism and Hinduism included. The bell symbolizes wisdom. At the moment, our wisdom bell is lying unused within us. The ring of the ritual bell is a reminder: "Use your wisdom!"

Q. Admittedly we should not be overly passive in our responsibilities, but sometimes taking karmic responsibility seems to heighten our sense of ego. There seems to be a choice between responsibility and outward energy as opposed to passive, inner wisdom.

Lama. Intellectually, we understand that there are the Buddha, Dharma and Sangha. This is positive. The Buddha is OK; Dharma is OK; Sangha is OK. But what is Buddha to me? When I totally develop myself, I become a buddha; that is *my* buddha. Shakyamuni Buddha is *his* buddha, not mine. He's gone. My total awakening is my buddha. How do you awaken to your own buddha? The first step is simply to be aware of the actions of your body, speech and mind. Of course, you should not be egotistical about it, thinking, "The Buddha and the Dharma are OK, but I don't care about them—I am responsible." And also you should not have pride: "I am a meditator." The whole point is to eradicate the ego—don't worry about whether you are a meditator or not. Just put your mind in the right channel, don't intellectualize, and let go. Your question is very good: we have to know how to deal with that mind. Thank you.

Q. You said that suicide rates are higher in the West than in the East. But it is also true that death from starvation is commoner in the East than in the West. It seems to be instinctive for the Easterner to renounce whereas materialism appears to be natural for Westerners. So may I suggest, skeptically, that renunciation has led the East to poverty while materialism has brought the West to affluence?

Lama. That's also a very good question. But remember what I said before: renouncing this glass does not mean throwing it away, breaking it or giving it to somebody else. You can eat your rice and *dal* with a renounced mind. It's very important for you to know that.

It's true that most Eastern people are culturally influenced by their religious tenets. For example, even when we are three or four years old, we accept the law of karma. Then again, most Eastern people also misunderstand karma. Somebody thinks, "Oh, I'm a

poor person, my father is a sweeper—I too have to be a sweeper."
"Why?" "Because it's my karma—it has to be that way."

This is a total misconception and has nothing to do with the teachings of either Hinduism or Buddhism; it's a fixed idea totally opposite to the nature of reality. We should understand, "I'm a human being—my nature is impermanent. Maybe I'm unhappy now, but I'm changeable—I can develop within myself the mind of eternal peace and joy." *This* is the attitude we should have.

The incredible changes we see in the world today come from the human mind, not from the world itself; the affluence of the materialistic West comes from the Western mind. If we Easterners want our standard of living to equal that of the West, we can do it. At the same time, however, we can have renunciation of samsara.

In order to develop renunciation, you have to understand the actual value of material goods and their relationship to happiness. Most Westerners grossly exaggerate the value of material things. They are bombarded with advertisements: "This gives you satisfaction;" "That gives you satisfaction"; "The other gives you satisfaction." So they become psychologically convinced, "I must buy this, I must buy that, otherwise I won't be happy." This conviction leads them to the extreme of materialism—and ultimately to suicide. Similarly, Easterners misconceive the teachings of religion and fall into the extreme of passivity, laziness and apathy: "Karma—it's my karma."

Q. What is the difference between *moksha* and nirvana?

Lama. There are several levels of moksha, or liberation. One of these is nirvana, which is beyond ego and is endowed with everlasting peace and bliss. Higher than nirvana is enlightenment, which is sometimes called the "great nirvana" and is the fruition of bodhicitta, the determination to reach enlightenment for the sole purpose of enlightening all the infinite sentient beings. You can lose interest in samsara, undergo spiritual training and attain nirvana, but you have yet to develop bodhicitta and realize full enlightenment.

Q. You spoke about non-duality. Do love and hate still exist in that state?

Lama. The experience of non-duality itself is in the nature of love. The emotional tone of love is lower during meditative absorption on non-duality but its nature is essentially present. Most people's love is biased and dualistic. Love characterized by non-duality feels no partiality. The lam-rim teaches us to meditate on how every single sentient being—including animals, birds, fish and insects— has repeatedly been a mother to us in our infinite previous lives. Moreover, without exception, they all want happiness and seek to avoid suffering. If we meditate and expand our objects of knowledge, we'll come to know the nature of other beings and our love will become vast.

Q. Nirvana seems to be a duality because it implies non-nirvana.

Lama. Linguistically, this is true. If we label something "nirvana," we create an entrance for the label "non-nirvana." But in the minds of those perceiving non-duality, there are no labels. They just experience nirvana and let themselves go into it.

Q. I always visualize nirvana as the LSD experience.

Lama. Then I guess there's not much nirvana here in the East.

Lama Yeshe (1935–84) was born and educated in Tibet. He fled the Chinese occupation in 1959 and continued his study and practice in India. In 1969 he and Lama Zopa Rinpoche began teaching at Kopan Monastery, Nepal. In 1974 they started traveling to the West and in 1975 founded the Foundation for the Preservation of the Mahayana Tradition. Lama Yeshe gave this teaching at Tushita Mahayana Meditation Centre, New Delhi, 31 October 1979. It was first published in *Teachings at Tushita* in 1981.

IN SEARCH OF
A MEANINGFUL LIFE

Lama Zopa Rinpoche

Inner development and materialism

IT IS EXTREMELY important that we make an effort to lead a spiritual life while, as human beings, we have the opportunity to pursue the inner methods that bring peace of mind.

It is common experience that happiness does not arise from external factors alone. If we check carefully into our own daily lives, we will easily see that this is true. In addition to external factors, there are also inner factors that come into play to establish happiness within us.

If external development were all it took to produce lasting peace within us, then those who were rich in material possessions would have more peace and happiness while those who were poor would have less. But life is not always like this. There are many happy people with few riches and many wealthy people who are very unhappy.

In India, for example, there are many pandits, highly realized yogis and even simple Dharma practitioners who live humble lives but have great peace of mind. The more they have renounced the unsubdued mind, the greater their peace; the more they have renounced self-cherishing, anger, ignorance, attachment and so forth, the greater their happiness.

Great masters such as the Indian pandit Naropa and the Tibetan yogi Jetsun Milarepa owned nothing yet had incredible peace of mind. They were able to renounce the unsubdued mind, the source of all problems, and thus transcended all suffering. By actualizing the path to enlightenment they achieved a superior happiness. Thus, even though they often had to go days without food—the great yogi Milarepa lived for years in a cave subsisting only on wild nettles—they rank among the happiest people on earth. Because they abandoned the three poisonous minds of ignorance, attachment and anger, their peace and happiness were indeed great. The more they renounced the unsubdued mind, the greater was their peace.

If happiness depended on only material development, rich countries such as America would be very happy places. Many people try to follow the American way of life, thinking it will bring them happiness, but personally, I find greater peace in more spiritually minded countries such as India and Nepal. These are much happier countries, more peaceful for the mind. When I return to India after traveling in the West, it's like coming home. There are so many differences. India is actually a very spiritual country and this makes a great difference to the mind.

When you look at materialistic societies and the way people live, your own mind gets disturbed. The people there are increasingly busy, and new and different problems continually arise; they're tense and nervous and have no time to relax. In India, you see people relaxing all over the place, but in the West, you pick up the vibration of the population's agitated minds and finish up feeling nervous yourself. If happiness depended solely on external development, countries like Switzerland and America would be the most peaceful places on earth, with less quarreling, fighting and violence, but they're not like that.

This proves that there is something lacking in the way the West seeks happiness. Materially developed countries may be on top of the world but many problems continue to destroy their peace and happiness. What is missing? It is inner development; external development is pursued to the exclusion of inner development, development of the mind. It's a huge mistake to focus solely on material progress while ignoring development of the mind, the good heart. This is the world's greatest mistake.

In itself, material progress is not bad and is to be encouraged, but inner development is much more important. You can't even compare the two—inner development is a trillion times more effective than external development in producing lasting happiness. You'll find neither peace nor happiness if you neglect to develop the mind. The good heart brings peace of mind. By all means, develop the material world, but at the same time, develop the mind. If you compare the peace of mind gained through material things to that generated by the good heart—by compassion, love, patience, and the elimination of the violent, unsubdued mind—the superior value of the latter is overwhelming.

PATIENCE VS. ANGER

Even if you owned a pile of diamonds the size of this earth, the peace you'd get from that would be minimal and could never compare with that afforded by inner development. No matter how many jewels you own, you're still beset by mental problems such as anger, attachment and so forth. If somebody insults you, for example, you immediately get angry and start to think of ways to harm, insult or hurt that person.

If you are a person of inner development, you react quite differently. You think, "How would I feel if he got angry with me, insulted me and hurt my mind? I'd be really upset and unhappy. Therefore, I shouldn't be negative toward him. If I get angry and insult him, he'll get terribly upset and unhappy, just as I would in the same situation. How can I do that to him?" This is the way you should think; this is the way of inner development, the true path to peace.

When your friend says or does something to you that you dislike and discomfort and anger start to grow in your mind, you may want to retaliate by saying something hurtful. But instead, you should gather your awareness, be skillful and brave, and think, "How can I be angry with my friend? How can I say painful things to her? How can I bring her harm? If she got violent with me, how unhappy I would be, how it would disturb my mind, how it would hurt me. Therefore, to harm this friend who, just like me, wants happiness and does not want suffering would be most shameful. What kind of person would I be if I acted like that?"

When we think like that, our anger, which at first seems to be as solid as stone, disappears like a popped water bubble. At first it seems that there's no way we can change our mind, but when we use the right method, when we meditate like this, our anger vanishes, just like that. We don't see the point of getting angry.

When we practice patience, we try not to let our anger arise; we try to remember how it disturbs our mind, destroys our happiness, disturbs others' minds and happiness, and doesn't help at all. As we practice patience, our face becomes beautiful. Anger makes us really ugly. When anger enters a beautiful face, no amount of make-up can hide the complete ugliness that manifests. We can see anger in people's faces; we can recognize it. We become afraid of anger just be looking at the terrifying face of an angry person. That is the reflection of anger. It's a very bad vibration to give off. It makes everybody unhappy.

The real practice of Dharma, the real meditation, is never to harm others. This protects both our own peace of mind and that of other beings. This is the true religious practice; it brings benefits to both others and ourselves. Practicing patience in this way even once is worth more than any amount of diamonds. What kind of inner peace can we derive from diamonds? All we do is run the risk of being killed for them. The value of the good heart is beyond compare with that of any material possession.

Since we want only happiness and no suffering, it is extremely important for us to practice Dharma. Dharma is not chanting, doing rituals or wearing uniforms; it's developing the mind, the inner factor. We have many different inner factors: negative ones, such as the unsubdued mind, ignorance, delusions and so forth; and positive ones, such as love, compassion, wisdom and the like. Dharma practice is the destruction of our negative mental factors and the cultivation of our positive ones.

Linguistically, the word "dharma" means "existent phenomenon," but when we say "the practice of Dharma" or "holy Dharma," it means that which protects us from suffering. That is the meaning of the holy Dharma; that is the Dharma we should practice.

There are many different levels of suffering from which we require protection. Dharma is like a rope thrown to somebody about to fall over a precipice. It protects and holds us from falling into the realms of suffering—the worlds of the hell beings, hungry ghosts and animals.

A second level of suffering from which the holy Dharma protects us is that of the entirety of samsaric suffering—that of all six realms—and its cause: the disturbing negative minds and the karma they cause us to create.

Finally, the holy Dharma also protects us from the self-cherishing thought and the subtle obscurations that prevent us from attaining enlightenment, the state of buddhahood—the highest sublime happiness. As long as the self-cherishing thought remains in our mind there's no way we can achieve buddhahood; the path to sublime happiness is blocked. Self-cherishing is the greatest hindrance to happiness and enlightenment. If we practice Dharma, we'll find protection from the disturbances that the self-cherishing thought creates and will quickly receive enlightenment.

Death is followed by the intermediate state, after which we take rebirth in one of the six realms. Rebirth, life, death, intermediate state, rebirth again: we constantly circle on this wheel of life, repeatedly experiencing confusion and suffering because of impure conceptions and views. When we practice Dharma, we're guided and protected from the impure conceptions and views that constantly keep us bound to samsaric suffering. Dharma practice helps us at many levels.

IDENTIFYING THE PROBLEM

The problem is that our body and mind are in the nature of suffering; they are not beyond suffering. This is the whole problem. As a result, we are constantly busy. Why is our body in the nature of suffering? It's because our mind is in the nature of suffering; our mind is not liberated from suffering because it is not liberated from the unsubdued minds of ignorance, attachment, anger and their actions, karma. Therefore, its nature is one of suffering. Thus, in turn, our body suffers too.

Without choice, our body is subject to the sufferings of heat, cold, hunger, thirst, birth, old age, sickness and so forth. We don't have to seek these sufferings out; they come to us naturally and we have to experience them. All this is because we have not liberated our mind from suffering. Our country is not samsara; our city is not samsara; our family is not samsara—samsara is the body and mind that are in the nature of suffering; the body and mind that constantly make us worry and keep us busy. Samsara is the body and mind that are bound by delusion and karma.

Samsara is a cycle, a wheel. Its function is to circle. How does it circle? Our aggregates—our body and mind—continue from this life into the next; they connect our past life to this one and this life to the future one. They always continue, always join one life to the next. They create an ongoing circle—like the wheels of a bicycle, they always take us to different places. We are the subject who circles, like the person who rides the bike. Our self is like that. We circle on and on, from life to life, taking rebirth in accordance with how we have lived our life—the karma we have created and our general state of mind. Dependent upon these factors, we take rebirth as an animal, a human, a god, a hell being and so forth. Our aggregates carry us like a horse carries a rider.

The problem is that from beginningless time throughout all our previous lives we did not do the work necessary to liberate our mind from the unsubdued mind and karma. Therefore, our mind and body are still in the nature of suffering; we're still experiencing the same problems over and over again. Had we liberated ourselves from the unsubdued mind and karma we would never have to suffer again; it would be impossible. Once we're free from samsaric suffering, from the bondage of karma and the unsubdued mind, we can never suffer again; no cause remains for us to experience further suffering. If we'd liberated ourselves before, there'd be no reason for us to suffer now; our mind and body would not be in the nature of suffering.

If we didn't have a samsaric body, we wouldn't need a house, clothing, food or other temporal needs. There'd be no need to worry, make preparations, collect many possessions, chase money, have hundreds of different clothes to wear in the different seasons, have hundreds of shoes, make business and so forth. We'd have none of these problems. But we do have a samsaric body, therefore our entire life, from rebirth to death, is kept busy taking care of it.

Lama Tsongkhapa, a highly realized Tibetan yogi recognized as an embodiment of Manjushri, the Buddha of Wisdom, wrote from his personal experience of the path,

> If you do not think of the evolution of samsara, you will not know how to sever its root.[18]

For example, let's say there's a person who is always sick because he eats the wrong food. As long as he doesn't recognize the mistake in his diet, the cause of his sickness, he will continue to be sick no matter how much medicine he takes. Similarly, if we don't understand the evolutionary patterns of samsara, there'll be no way for us to receive the peace of nirvana that we seek. To do this, we must cut the root of samsara; to do that, we must know the correct methods; to know the methods, we must recognize what causes us to be bound to samsara. By understanding what binds us to samsara, we can generate aversion for and renunciation of the causes of samsaric existence. Lama Tsongkhapa concludes the above verse by saying,

> I, the yogi, have practiced just that. You who also seek liberation, please cultivate yourself in the same way.

---

[18] "Lines of Experience," verse 13, appendix 2, in the Dalai Lama, *Illuminating the Path*.

This great yogi, who achieved enlightenment by actualizing the path, advises us to do what he did: first, it is very important that we desire liberation from samsara; then we must recognize its evolutionary laws; finally, we have to sever its root.

To understand the evolution of samsara we must understand the twelve links of dependent arising, or interdependent origination, that clearly explain how we circle in samsara.[19] How did our present samsara—these aggregates in the nature of suffering—come into being? In a past life, out of ignorance, we accumulated the karma to be born in this human body. A split second before our previous life's death, craving and grasping—not wanting to leave the body, not wanting to separate from that life—arose. We were then born in the intermediate state, and after that our consciousness entered our mother's womb. The resultant embryo grew and our senses gradually developed. Then contact and responsive feelings came into existence. Now our rebirth has occurred, we are aging, and all that remains for us to experience is death.

In this life there is no peace from the time we are born until the time we die. We continually go through much suffering as human beings: the pain of birth; dissatisfaction with our situation; undesirable experiences; worries; fear of separation from desirable objects, friends, relatives and possessions; sickness; old age and death. All these problems come from karma, and karma comes from ignorance. Therefore, the one root of samsara is ignorance, the ignorance of mistaking the nature of I, the self, which is empty of true existence—although our I is empty of true existence, we completely believe that it is truly existent, as we project. By totally eradicating this ignorance, we put a final end to our beginningless suffering and attain nirvana.

---

[19] See Geshe Rabten's teaching on the twelve links, p. 137

THE PATH THAT REPAYS THE KINDNESS OF ALL
SENTIENT BEINGS

In order to put an end to our suffering, we must follow a true path. However, it is not enough that we ourselves attain nirvana because that benefits only one person. There are numberless sentient beings, all of whom have been our mother, father, sister and brother in our infinite previous lives. There is not one single sentient being who has not been kind to us in one life or another. Even in this life, much of our happiness is received in dependence upon the kindness of others, not only humans. For example, many animals work hard and suffer for our happiness; many die or are killed for us. In order to produce rice in a field, many people work and suffer under the sun, many creatures are killed and so forth. The happiness of each day of our life completely depends on the kindness of other sentient beings.

As human beings, we have a great opportunity to repay their kindness. They are ignorant of and blind to Dharma wisdom but since we have met the holy Dharma, we're able to understand the nature of reality and help all sentient beings by reaching enlightenment and liberating them from suffering. Therefore, we should always think as follows:

> I must attain enlightenment in order to benefit all sentient beings. Sentient beings have been extremely kind and benefited me very much. They are suffering. These sentient beings, all of whom have been my mother in countless previous lives, are suffering. Therefore I, their child, must help. If I don't help them, who will? Who else will help them gain liberation from suffering? Who else will lead them to enlightenment? But for me to do that, I must first reach enlightenment myself; I must become a buddha; I must actualize the omniscient mind. Then my holy body, speech and mind will become most effective.

Each ray of light from the aura of the enlightened holy body can liberate many sentient beings and inspire them on the path to happiness, nirvana and full enlightenment. I must become a buddha in order to liberate all sentient beings.

The path is the holy Dharma and the essence of the path is the good heart. The greatest, highest good heart is bodhicitta—the determination to become a buddha in order to liberate all sentient beings from suffering. This is the supreme good heart. This is what we should generate.

Lama Zopa Rinpoche (1945–) was born in Nepal and lived in Tibet from 1956–59, when he fled the Chinese occupation for India, where he met Lama Yeshe. He started teaching Westerners with Lama Yeshe at Kopan Monastery and internationally, and when Lama passed away in 1984 Rinpoche became head of the FPMT, which has flourished under his peerless leadership. Rinpoche gave this teaching at Tushita Mahayana Meditation Centre, New Delhi, 4 July 1979. It was first published in *Teachings at Tushita* in 1981.

How to Start Practicing Dharma

Zong Rinpoche

PRACTICING DHARMA IS A PERSONAL CHOICE

GENERALLY SPEAKING, it's up to you as an individual whether or not you practice Dharma. It's not something you can be forced to do—unless it's the law of the land, in which case everybody has to do it. But even then, it's not really practicing Dharma because adhering to the law of the land is done just for this life.

If you live just for this life, you don't benefit your future lives, whereas if you practice Dharma, you bring happiness to not only all your future lives but your present life as well.

However, you have to find and practice the right Dharma; if you practice the wrong Dharma, no matter how much you do it, you'll just waste your whole life.

I don't need to explain why you need to practice Dharma; I think you understand that. Various religions have appeared on this earth but Guru Shakyamuni Buddha's Dharma offers happiness and benefit at the beginning, in the middle and at the end. Its cause is virtue, it results in virtue, it creates virtue all the time and, therefore, brings continual benefit.

Originally, Buddhadharma spread widely throughout India and later went to Tibet. These days, because of unfavorable conditions, the Dharma is again spreading in India and even beyond. I use the word "unfavorable" because the conditions I'm referring to are the ones that destroyed Buddhism in Tibet. However, since these same conditions have helped Dharma spread to other countries, from that point of view perhaps they're not so unfavorable.

What should you do when you encounter Dharma? First you should listen, then try to understand the meaning and, finally, meditate. If you practice in that way, you can attain enlightenment.

There are two reasons for listening to teachings: one is simply to gain intellectual understanding; the other is to know how to practice. If you practice Dharma, it will get rid of disturbing negative thoughts and transform your mind; change it for the better. This brings you happiness in this and future lives.

If you listen to the Dharma to gain an intellectual understanding but don't put the teachings you hear into practice, you don't benefit your mind that much. However, since what you're listening to is Buddhadharma, there is *some* benefit—hearing the teachings leaves imprints on your consciousness; it plants seeds in your mind. Then, in a future life, you'll more easily be able to understand and realize the Dharma.

Therefore, if you are listening to teachings in order to understand and meditate on them, that's excellent, but even if you're simply trying to gain an intellectual understanding, that, too, creates extensive merit and is a cause for rejoicing. Whatever your motivation for thinking about the Dharma, you should feel, "How greatly fortunate I am."

Since we have met the Dharma in these degenerate times, it's extremely important that we do not waste this opportunity. Once you've begun to practice, it's essential that you not only continue to do so but that you also complete your practice. First try to understand the teachings; then try to make what you've understood as beneficial as possible for other sentient beings.

In order to develop Dharma in your mind, you must find a perfectly qualified guru. These days, there are a number of learned monks, geshes and lamas outside of Tibet—far more than there are in Tibet itself. In Tibet there's no longer any freedom in either the material life or Dharma practice; what used to be has been completely destroyed.

His Holiness the Dalai Lama has taken upon himself the great responsibility of trying to guide the Tibetan people in exile both materially and spiritually. If he is not successful in gaining independence for Tibet, the teachings will really be in danger of getting lost, because many of the highly realized lamas are now quite elderly and will soon pass away.[20] If His Holiness is successful, the Dharma may again spread throughout Tibet, which will also be of great benefit to the rest of the world. The redevelopment and preservation of the Dharma in Tibet is of enormous importance, so please pray that all His Holiness's holy wishes will be fulfilled.

That which we call Dharma is medicine to treat the mind, to change it from its unsubdued, pre-Dharma state to a better one. From beginningless time our mind has been stained, foggy, polluted and disturbed by the three poisons of ignorance, attachment and anger because we have either not understood or not practiced the teachings. Dharma is medicine to change that kind of mind for the better.

REINCARNATION

Buddhism isn't the only religion that teaches rebirth. In ancient India, for example, there were many non-Buddhist faiths that believed in reincarnation.[21] But one of these religions—the Charvakas (Hedonists),[22] whose view was particularly limited—denied the existence of rebirth because they believed that only things that you can see with your eye exist. That was their logic: if you can see it, it exists; if you can't, it doesn't. Even ordinary people would agree that this is an extremely limited, ignorant view. There are many things that you can't see—like the back of your head, things buried underground or what other people are thinking—but they still exist.

There are many reasons proving the existence of past and future lives, but if you haven't studied the extensive texts that go into those reasons, it's difficult for me to explain them and for you to understand.

[20] Note that this teaching was given in 1978.
[21] See Hopkins, *Meditation on Emptiness,* 317–33, for a discussion of non-Buddhist systems.
[22] Zong Rinpoche refers to them by one of their other names, Yang-pän-pa (Skt: Ayata). See Hopkins, *Meditation on Emptiness,* 327–30, for a discussion of this system.

However, since you are already interested in the practice of Dharma, it's not imperative that I try to explain the existence of reincarnation to you. Anyway, the number of existent phenomena that we can't see is vastly greater than the number of things we can; there's basically no comparison. The things that we don't see or realize are countless; our present knowledge is almost zero. Just that shows how little we know.

What you need to know to practice Dharma

Probably the best thing you can do to practice Dharma is to follow the teachings on the three scopes of the graduated path to enlightenment: the paths for those of small, medium and higher potential, or capability. By practicing the teachings, you can generate the three principal aspects of the path—renunciation of samsara, bodhicitta and the right view of emptiness—which qualifies you to follow the graduated path of secret mantra, or the Vajrayana.

However, the main thing you should do is train your mind in bodhicitta, because without this, there's not the slightest possibility of attaining the blissful state of enlightenment; you absolutely must engage in the great practices of the Mahayana thought transformation. Without training in bodhicitta, you're not even permitted to listen to teachings on tantra, let alone put them into practice. And when you do enter the path of tantra, you should keep your practice secret; that's why the tantric teachings are also called secret mantra.

Not only can the teachings of secret mantra not be explained to those whose minds are unripe and unreceptive; even the teachings of the great Mahayana thought transformation should not be revealed to those whose minds are not ready. You can't just go out into the middle of town and give them to any passerby. In fact, they should be given only to students who sincerely ask their teacher for them.

If you want to attain enlightenment, you need to practice tantra, and to do that, you need to train your mind in bodhicitta. In order to train in bodhicitta, you need to practice the great Mahayana thought transformation, and to do that, you need to receive teachings on it. Therefore, you should sincerely request your teacher for teachings on the stages of the path, especially those on thought transformation. Then, even if your mind has not become bodhicitta, if it's close to bodhicitta, you can receive initiations and teachings on secret mantra, which is extremely beneficial; this leaves a great impression on your mind.

Before you receive teachings on the great Mahayana thought transformation, you need to study the preliminary teachings on the graduated path to enlightenment.

The purpose of Dharma is to subdue your mind, to correct the actions of your daily life so that they become beneficial. So, Dharma teachings are a mirror that clearly reflects the actions of your body, speech and mind so that you can judge whether they are beneficial—the cause of happiness—or harmful—the cause of suffering.

Since beginningless previous lives, we have been under the control of disturbing negative thoughts, which have forced us to constantly create, without choice, harmful actions, negative karma, the cause of suffering. As a result, since beginningless time, we have been experiencing the various sufferings of samsara and, even in this life, we continue to do so. From the time of our birth, we've not had one day free of problems.

In other words, we're sick; we're patients. We're suffering from the disease of the disturbing negative thoughts, which cause us to create mistaken actions, which bring the result of suffering. What can cure this illness? What can alleviate our suffering? What treatment do we need? It's Dharma. Dharma is the only medicine that can help.

Now, the thing about medicine is that it has to be taken. The patient who has the right medicine but doesn't take it doesn't get cured. Similarly, if we don't practice the Dharma teachings we receive, we can't put an end to the problems of our daily life or escape from suffering.

Before receiving teachings on the great Mahayana thought transformation, we need to accomplish the preliminary practices. These are the right foundation for the meditations on bodhicitta. These initial teachings include those on the perfect human rebirth—what it is, how meaningful it is and how difficult it will be to receive again; impermanence and death; refuge in Buddha, Dharma and Sangha; karma; and the shortcomings of cyclic existence. You should begin your practice by studying and then putting into practice the teachings on the perfect human rebirth.

His Holiness Zong Rinpoche (1905–84) was born in Kham, Tibet, studied at Ganden Monastery, gained renown as a learned geshe and great debater and served as abbot for nine years. He fled Tibet for India in 1959 and in 1967 was appointed as the first principal of the new Central Institute of Higher Tibetan Studies (now the Central University for Tibetan Studies) in Sarnath. Rinpoche gave this introductory teaching on the first day of a two-week course on Mahayana thought transformation at Camp Kennolyn, Soquel, California, 20 May 1978, during his first trip to the West. It was translated by Lama Zopa Rinpoche and is forthcoming as a book by LYWA.

ADVICE ON GURU PRACTICE

Gomchen Khampala

Lama Thubten Zopa Rinpoche's introduction: Gomchen-la is a great meditator from the mountains of Solu Khumbu not far from where I was born. He's originally from Tibet. He rejoices greatly that Western people are saying prayers and meditating on the Buddhadharma because it's unusual, not normal. It's as if the impossible has happened. Therefore, he rejoices. I have asked him to give the Western students some instruction, and it seems he has much energy to do so. He's also saying that I should translate everything he says and not hold anything back!

I HAVE SPENT ONLY one night at Kopan, but the feeling here is very good. I think it's because everybody is living in refuge; it's the power of people's minds living in refuge and their becoming inner beings, or Buddhists.

In Lama Zopa Rinpoche's previous life he lived in Solu Khumbu as the Lawudo Lama, and at that time you were also probably born around that area and made karmic contact with him. Because of that and your good fortune as well, even though in this life you were born in far-distant foreign countries, you have found a teacher who can explain Dharma in your own language, which other lamas can't do. Therefore, you are greatly fortunate. You should take this opportunity and, in particular, take great care with your guru practice.

There are many lamas from the different schools—Nyingma, Kagyü, Gelug and Sakya—who can explain the Dharma very well, but the problem is language.

In Buddhadharma, guru practice is the most important thing. In fact, the only object to whom we need pray is the guru, because the guru encompasses the entire Triple Gem—Buddha, Dharma and Sangha. Therefore, first of all, it is necessary to find a perfect guru, but I'm not going to talk about that here.

In the sutra teachings, we take refuge in Buddha, Dharma and

Sangha, but in tantra, we take refuge in the guru. As it says in the *Guru Puja*,

> You are my guru, you are my yidam,
> You are the dakinis and Dharma protectors.
> From now until enlightenment,
> I shall seek no refuge other than you.

This is the tantric way of taking refuge. You should try to actualize this; gain experience of it. Lama Zopa Rinpoche should explain this practice to you and from your side you should make heartfelt requests to receive teachings on the practice of guru yoga.

When I was in Tibet I asked my guru to explain it to me but he said, "If I talk about guru practice it will look as if I'm praising myself; as if I'm saying, 'I am good; I am the best,'" and would not explain it to me. He told me, "You can study the details of guru practice in books to understand what it entails. If the lama explains it the disciples might think he's just aggrandizing himself or boasting that he's the best."

I rejoice that you are not only reciting prayers but analyzing the meaning of the teachings as well; thinking of the meaning and concentrating on the fundamental path. Say that there were many millions of billions of galaxies full of stupas full of Buddha's relics and every day you made offerings to all of them, there would be enormous benefit in that. But as it says in the Mahamudra teachings, "Meditating on the fundamental path for just a short time has more benefit than every day making offerings to millions of billions of galaxies full of stupas containing relics of the Buddha." Therefore, I thank Lama Zopa Rinpoche and all of you.

There are many people who can recite the words and give clear intellectual explanations of the teachings but don't practice or analyze the meaning. Here, you are doing both: not only are you thinking about what the words mean but at the same time you are trying to put that meaning into practice. Study combined with meditation—meditating while receiving the teaching—is called "experiencing the commentary"—while the teacher is giving the commentary the disciples try to gain experience of it. That's a wise and excellent way to practice.

There's a prayer of request to the guru that goes,

> Magnificent and precious root guru,
> Please abide on the lotus and moon seat at the crown
>   of my head.
> Guide me with your great kindness,
> And grant me the realizations of your holy body, speech
>   and mind.

What is the kindness to which this prayer refers? It's what's happening here at Kopan Monastery, being guided by the guru, who out of his great kindness gives commentaries on the teachings and confers initiations, which ripen the mind.

With respect to the last line of this prayer, the essence of whatever deity you're meditating on—for example, Avalokiteshvara—is the guru. Meditational deities are manifestations of the guru. When we request the realizations of our guru's holy body, speech and mind, we receive the blessings of the guru's holy body, speech and mind. These blessings purify the negativities of our own body, speech and mind, which then become one with our guru's holy body, speech and mind.

Once, the great pandit and yogi Naropa was reading texts in the extensive library of a great temple when a dakini suddenly appeared out of a dark cloud in the space in front of him and said, "You know the words but you don't know the meaning."

"Where can I learn the meaning?" Naropa asked.

She replied, "There's a great yogi called Tilopa. You can receive the commentaries from him."

Consequently, as directed by the dakini, the great pandit Naropa went to West Bengal, in the northeastern part of India, in search of his guru, Tilopa. When he got there, he asked the local people if they knew Tilopa. They said, "There are two Tilopas: a rich one and a poor one, a beggar. There are two." Naropa said, "Tilopa, the guru I have to find, doesn't necessarily have to be rich or poor."

Later, as he went around, he found Tilopa by the river, pulling fish from the water, cooking them over a fire and eating them. Seeing this, instead of criticizing Tilopa or being shocked by his behavior, he remained silent; not a hair of his body moved. He just stood there quietly, without a single negative or disparaging thought, and simply reflected, "Since sentient beings are so ignorant, in order to release them from ignorance and lead them to enlightenment, Tilopa has manifested in this form, catching fish and eating them."

Thinking like this is one way of practicing guru yoga. In previous lifetimes, Naropa had created the incredible merit and karma necessary to meet a guru such as Tilopa and never generate a single negative thought about him. Therefore, when he finally did meet this great guru, he realized he was a true saint and saw him in only a positive light. Similarly, you people have also created good karma in previous lives. In fact, your karma might be even better than Naropa's was because you see your guru in a better aspect—as a monk in robes.

Anyway, when Naropa saw Tilopa, he said, "Please guide me," meaning, "Please lead me to enlightenment."

At first, Tilopa replied, "I'm just a simple beggar, I can't do it; I can't accept your request. I can't help you." But finally he did accept, after which Naropa followed his guru impeccably.

One day while they were walking along the edge of a high cliff, Tilopa said, "Is there anybody here who can fulfill the guru's command?" which is the way to become enlightened in the one lifetime. The command was to leap off the cliff.

Naropa replied, "None other than me can do it, so I will," and he threw himself over the cliff.

He lay there at the foot of the cliff, badly injured, for three days, during which time Tilopa completely ignored him. Finally Tilopa asked Naropa, "What happened? What's wrong with you?"

"This is the result of following the guru's orders," Naropa said. Then, just by Tilopa's laying his hand on Naropa, all his injuries were completely healed.

Naropa underwent twelve such life-threatening experiences following his guru's orders. It would take too long to recount them here and anyway, I'm quite old and don't remember them very well.

Another time, Tilopa told Naropa to go get some soup from some farmers working in a field. They wouldn't give him any so he tried to steal some, but they caught him and beat him very badly. Again, Tilopa just left him lying there for three days, after which time he asked, "What's up with you?"

The whole point is that without a single exception, Naropa did exactly what his guru told him to do. Like the time they came across a royal wedding, where a king was getting married. There was a magnificent procession with the bride on horseback. Tilopa said, "The disciple who wants enlightenment in this life should go grab that bride." Naropa thought, "That's me," and without any hesitation or doubt went straight up to the wedding party, pulled the woman off the horse and tried to drag her away. All the people immediately jumped on Naropa, bashed him up and even cut off some of his limbs.

Again, Tilopa left him for three days and finally returned to ask, "What's the matter with you?"

"This happened because I followed my guru's orders." Once more Tilopa healed Naropa just by touching him and his severed limbs were miraculously restored.

There's another story about the day that Tilopa hit Naropa on the head with his shoe so strongly that he passed out. When Naropa came to, his mind and his guru's holy mind had become one; whatever knowledge Tilopa had, so did Naropa. This was the result of his impeccable guru devotion and doing exactly what Tilopa told him to do.

As the teachings explain, you have to decide completely that the guru is definitely buddha. If you don't come to that conclusion, then no matter what Dharma practices you do, they won't be of much benefit; they won't become a quick path to enlightenment.

Another teaching says, "Meditating on the guru's holy body is hundreds of thousands of times more powerful than meditating on trillions of deities in all their various aspects." However, whatever deity you meditate on, you have to remember, "This is my guru's holy body." You should not think, "This is the deity; the guru is something else."

Also, following your guru's instructions is far more beneficial than reciting the deity's mantra trillions of times.

There are two stages of the Highest Yoga Tantra path to enlightenment: generation and completion. While there is great benefit in meditating on the completion stage, doing it for even many eons pales in comparison to invoking the guru's holy mind just once.

I don't have that much more to say. I just wanted to say a few words about guru practice, so I'm simply emphasizing a few of the important points.

As I mentioned, you should request Lama Zopa Rinpoche for teachings on guru devotion and from your side pray to the guru as one with the deity. But remember what my guru told me when I asked for teachings on guru practice: "You can understand the practice of guru devotion by reading the texts; if I explain it to you, it will appear as if I'm extolling my own virtues; boasting that I'm the best of all."

These days, people can't practice like the great pandits of old. It's very difficult. Instead of following our gurus' orders like those fortunate beings did we have a bad attitude toward our teachers; instead of generating devotion, we criticize them; instead of doing what they suggest, we do the opposite.

However, even though we can't practice like those great pandits did—purifying their negativities by following their gurus' orders—we can purify in other ways. For example, we can do prostrations, make mandala offerings, recite Vajrasattva mantras and so forth.

There are many different tantric deities but in essence all of them are the guru. Therefore, when we make offerings to the various deities, we are actually making offerings to the guru.

The way to receive blessings is not to think that Avalokiteshvara is separate from your guru but that they are one. The really quick way to receive blessings is to concentrate on the guru and make your mind one with his holy mind, like mixing water with milk.

Don't think that Avalokiteshvara is somewhere else, is more beautiful than your guru or has no relationship to the guru from whom you receive teachings. It is not like that. Avalokiteshvara, or any other deity, *is* the guru. This is what I really want to emphasize.

There was once a yogi called Tsang-nyön-pa. Tsang is the name of a place; *nyön* means crazy. This yogi led an ascetic life and wandered around a lot. Before eating, he would always offer his food to his guru. One day he was in a forest and met a shepherd, who gave him some *tsampa*. He hadn't eaten for a long time and was very hungry, so he started eating it immediately. But the moment he put the food into his mouth, he thought, "Oh, I forgot to offer it." So he took the tsampa out of his mouth and, with incredible devotion, offered it to his guru.

At that moment his guru was giving teachings many miles away. All of a sudden, the food that Tsang-nyön-pa offered appeared in his guru's mouth and he had to stop speaking. He said, "Today my disciple Tsang-nyön-pa, who hadn't eaten for a long time, got some tsampa and offered it to me with such great devotion and single-pointed concentration that it actually came into my mouth."

The amount of Dharma you know, the number of realizations you gain, depends on how much devotion you have for your guru—the greater your devotion, the greater your Dharma understanding and realizations. It all depends on guru devotion.

The great meditator Ngawang Norbu Gomchen Khampala (ca. 1901–85) was the incarnation of the renowned fifteenth century Tibetan lama, Tangtong Gyälpo—*mahasiddha*, healer, scholar, poet and scientist. He invented a method of forging steel and developed chain-link bridges in Tibet. He lived in a cave high in the mountains of Solu Khumbu, Nepal, and on 10 January 1975, on a visit to Kopan Monastery, gave the following teaching to students in a lam-rim retreat and the monks and nuns of the International Mahayana Institute. It was translated by Lama Zopa Rinpoche.

THE FOUR NOBLE TRUTHS

His Holiness the Dalai Lama

WHEN THE GREAT universal teacher Shakyamuni Buddha first spoke about the Dharma in the noble land of India, he taught the four noble truths: the truths of suffering, the cause of suffering, the cessation of suffering and the path to the cessation of suffering. Since many books contain discussions of the four noble truths in English, these truths (as well as the eightfold path) are very well known. These four are all encompassing, including many things within them.

Considering the four noble truths in general and the fact that none of us wants suffering and we all desire happiness, we can speak of an effect and a cause on both the disturbing side and the liberating side. True sufferings and true causes are the effect and cause on the side of things that we do not want; true cessation and true paths are the effect and cause on the side of things that we desire.

THE TRUTH OF SUFFERING

We experience many different types of suffering. All are included in three categories: the suffering of suffering, the suffering of change and all-pervasive suffering.

Suffering of suffering refers to things such as headaches and so forth. Even animals recognize this kind of suffering and, like us, want to be free from it. Because beings have fear of and experience discomfort from these kinds of suffering, they engage in various activities to eliminate them.

Suffering of change refers to situations where, for example, we are sitting very comfortably relaxed and, at first, everything seems all right but after a while we lose that feeling and get restless and uncomfortable.

In certain countries we see a great deal of poverty and disease: these are sufferings of the first category. Everybody realizes that these are suffering conditions to be eliminated and improved upon. In many Western countries, poverty may not be that much of a problem, but where there is a high degree of material development there are different kinds of problems. At first we may be happy having overcome the problems that our predecessors faced, but as soon as we have solved certain problems, new ones arise. We have plenty of money, plenty of food and nice housing, but by exaggerating the value of these things we render them ultimately worthless. This sort of experience is the suffering of change.

A very poor, underprivileged person might think that it would be wonderful to have a car or a television set and, should he acquire them, would at first feel very happy and satisfied. Now, if such happiness were permanent, as long as he had the car and the TV set he would remain happy. But he does not; his happiness goes away. After a few months he wants another kind of car; if he has the money, he will buy a better television set. The old things, the same objects that once gave him much satisfaction, now cause dissatisfaction. That is the nature of change; that is the problem of the suffering of change.

All-pervasive suffering[23] is the third type of suffering. It is called all-pervasive because it acts as the basis of the first two.

There may be those who, even in developed countries, want to be liberated from the second suffering, the suffering of change. Bored with the defiled feelings of happiness, they seek the feeling of equanimity, which can lead to rebirth in the formlessness realm that has only that feeling.

Now, desiring liberation from the first two categories of suffering is not the principal motivation for seeking liberation from cyclic existence; the Buddha taught that the root of the three sufferings is the third: all-pervasive suffering. Some people commit suicide; they seem to think that there is suffering simply because there is human

---

[23] Tib: *kyab-pa du-che kyi dug-ngäl*—literally, the suffering of pervasive compounding.

life and that by ending their life there will be nothing. This third, all-pervasive, suffering is under the control of karma and the disturbing mind. We can see without having to think very deeply that this is under the control of the karma and disturbing mind of previous lives: anger and attachment arise simply because we have these present aggregates. The aggregate of compounding phenomena is like an enabler for us to generate karma and these disturbing minds; this is called *nä-ngän-len*.[24] Because that which forms is related to taking the bad place of disturbing minds and is under their control, it supports our generating disturbing minds and keeps us from virtue. All our suffering can be traced back to these aggregates of attachment and clinging.

Perhaps, when you realize that your aggregates are the cause of all your suffering, you might think that suicide is the way out. Well, if there were no continuity of mind, no future life, all right—if you had the courage you could finish yourself off. But according to the Buddhist viewpoint, that's not the case; your consciousness will continue. Even if you take your own life, this life, you will have to take another body that will again be the basis of suffering. If you really want to get rid of all your suffering, all the difficulties you experience in your life, you have to get rid of the fundamental cause that gives rise to the aggregates that are the basis of all suffering. Killing yourself isn't going to solve your problems.

Because this is the case, we must now investigate the cause of suffering: is there a cause or not? If there is, what kind of cause is it: a natural cause, which cannot be eliminated, or a cause that depends on its own cause and therefore can be? If it is a cause that can be overcome, is it possible for us to overcome it? Thus we come to the second noble truth, the truth of the cause of suffering.

[24] Literally, "taking a bad place."

THE TRUTH OF THE CAUSE OF SUFFERING

Buddhists maintain that there is no external creator and that even though a buddha is the highest being, even a buddha does not have the power to create new life. So now, what is the cause of suffering?

Generally, the ultimate cause is the mind. The mind that is influenced by negative thoughts such as anger, attachment, jealousy and so forth is the main cause of birth and all such other problems. However, there is no possibility of ending the mind, of interrupting the stream of consciousness itself. Furthermore, there is nothing intrinsically wrong with the deepest level of mind; it is simply influenced by the negative thoughts. Thus, the question is whether or not we can fight and control anger, attachment and the other disturbing negative minds. If we can eradicate these, we shall be left with a pure mind that is free from the causes of suffering.

This brings us to the disturbing negative minds, the delusions, which are mental factors. There are many different ways of presenting the discussion of the mind, but in general, the mind itself is something that is mere clarity and awareness. When we speak of disturbing attitudes such as anger and attachment, we have to see how they are able to affect and pollute the mind; what, in fact, is their nature? This, then, is the discussion of the cause of suffering.

If we ask how attachment and anger arise, the answer is that they are undoubtedly assisted by our grasping at things to be true and inherently real. When, for instance, we are angry at something, we feel that the object is out there, solid, true and unimputed, and that we ourselves are likewise something solid and findable. Before we get angry, the object appears ordinary, but when our mind is influenced by anger, the object looks ugly, completely repulsive, nauseating; something we want to get rid of immediately—it appears to really exist in that way: solid, independent and very unattractive. This appearance of "truly ugly" fuels our anger. Yet when we see the same object the next day, when our anger has subsided, it seems more beautiful than it did the day before; it's the same object but it doesn't seem as bad. This shows how anger and attachment are influenced by our grasping at things as being true and unimputed.

Thus the texts on Middle Way philosophy state that the root of all the disturbing negative minds is grasping at true existence; that this assists them and brings them about; that the closed-minded ignorance that grasps at things as being inherently, truly real is the basic source of all our suffering. Based on this grasping at true existence we develop all kinds of disturbing negative minds and create a great deal of negative karma.

In his *Guide to the Middle Way*, the great Indian pandit Chandrakirti says that first there's attachment to the self, which is then followed by grasping at things and becoming attached to them as "mine." At first there is a very solid, independent I that is very big—bigger than anything else; this is the basis. From this gradually comes "this is mine; this is mine; this is mine." Then "we, we, we." Then, because of our taking this side, come "others, our enemies." Toward I and mine, attachment arises. Toward him, her and them, we feel distance and anger; then jealousy and all other competitive feelings arise. Thus ultimately, the problem is this feeling of I—not the mere I but the I with which we become obsessed. This gives rise to anger and irritation, along with harsh words and all the physical expressions of aversion and hatred.

All these negative actions of body, speech and mind accumulate bad karma. Killing, cheating and all similar negative actions also result from bad motivation. The first stage is solely mental, the disturbing negative minds; in the second stage these negative minds express themselves in actions, karma. Immediately, the atmosphere is disturbed. With anger, for example, the atmosphere becomes tense and people feel uneasy. If somebody gets furious, gentle people try to avoid that person. Later on, the person who got angry also feels embarrassed and ashamed for having said all sorts of absurd things, whatever came into his or her mind. When you get angry, there's no room for logic or reason; you become literally mad. Later, when your mind has returned to normal, you feel ashamed. There's nothing good about anger and attachment; nothing good can result from them. They may be difficult to control, but everybody can realize that there is nothing good about them. This, then, is the second noble truth. Now the question arises whether or not these kinds of negative mind can be eliminated.

THE TRUTH OF THE CESSATION OF SUFFERING

The root of all disturbing negative minds is our grasping at things as truly existent. Therefore, we have to investigate whether this grasping mind is correct or whether it is distorted and seeing things incorrectly. We can do this by investigating how the things it perceives actually exist. However, since this mind itself is incapable of seeing whether or not it apprehends objects correctly, we have to rely on another kind of mind. If, upon investigation, we discover many other, valid ways of looking at things and that all these contradict, or negate, the way that the mind that grasps at true existence perceives its objects, we can say that this mind does not see reality.

Thus, with the mind that can analyze the ultimate, we must try to determine whether the mind that grasps at things as truly findable is correct or not. If it is correct, the analyzing mind should ultimately be able to find the grasped-at things. The great classics of the Mind Only and, especially, the Middle Way schools contain many lines of reasoning for carrying out such investigation. Following these, when you investigate to see whether the mind that grasps at things as inherently findable is correct or not, you find that it is not correct, that it is distorted—you cannot actually find the objects at which it grasps. Since this mind is deceived by its object it has to be eliminated.

Thus, through investigation we find no valid support for the grasping mind but do find the support of logical reasoning for the mind that realizes that the grasping mind is invalid. In spiritual battle, the mind supported by logic is always victorious over the mind that is not. The understanding that there is no such thing as truly findable existence constitutes the deep clear nature of mind; the mind that grasps at things as truly findable is superficial and fleeting.

When we eliminate the disturbing negative minds, the cause of all suffering, we eliminate the sufferings as well. This is liberation, or the cessation of suffering: the third noble truth. Since it is possible to achieve this we must now look at the method. This brings us to the fourth noble truth.

THE TRUTH OF THE PATH TO THE CESSATION OF SUFFERING

When we speak of the paths common to the three vehicles of Buddhism—Hinayana, Mahayana and Vajrayana—we are referring to the thirty-seven factors that bring enlightenment. When we speak specifically of the paths of the Bodhisattvas' Vehicle we are referring to the ten levels and the six transcendent perfections.

We find the practice of the Hinayana path most commonly in Thailand, Burma, Sri Lanka and so forth. Here, practitioners are motivated by the desire to achieve liberation from their own suffering. Concerned for themselves alone, they practice the thirty-seven factors of enlightenment, which are related to the five paths: the four close placements of mindfulness, the four miraculous powers and the four pure abandonments (which are related to the path of accumulation); the five powers and the five forces (the path of preparation); the seven factors of enlightenment (the path of seeing); and the eightfold path (the path of meditation). In this way, they are able to completely cease the disturbing negative minds and attain individual liberation. This is the path and result of the Hinayana.

The primary concern of followers of the Mahayana path is not merely their own liberation but the enlightenment of all sentient beings. With this motivation of bodhicitta—their hearts set on attaining enlightenment as the best means of helping others—these practitioners practice the six transcendent perfections and gradually progress through the ten bodhisattva levels until they have completely overcome both types of obscurations and attained the supreme enlightenment of buddhahood. This is the path and the result of the Mahayana.

The essence of the practice of the six transcendent perfections is the unification of method and wisdom so that the two enlightened bodies—*rupakaya* and *dharmakaya*—can be attained. Since they can be attained only simultaneously, their causes must be cultivated simultaneously. Therefore, together we must build up a store of merit—as the cause of the rupakaya, the body of form—and a store of deep awareness, or insight—as the cause of the dharmakaya, the body of wisdom. In the Paramitayana, we practice method grasped by wisdom and wisdom grasped by method, but in the Vajrayana we practice method and wisdom as one in nature.

———————◆———————

The Dalai Lama gave this teaching in Dharamsala, 7 October 1981. It was translated by Alexander Berzin, clarified by Lama Zopa Rinpoche, edited by Nicholas Ribush and first published in the souvenir booklet for Tushita Mahayana Meditation Centre's Second Dharma Celebration, November 5–8, 1982, New Delhi, India.

Method, Wisdom and the Three Paths

Geshe Lhundub Sopa

ANDY KRAASHAUR

SEARCHING FOR HAPPINESS

THE GREAT eleventh century Indian master Atisha said,

> Human life is short,
> Objects of knowledge are many.
> Be like a swan,
> Which can separate milk from water.[25]

Our lives will not last long and there are many directions in which we can channel our energy. Just as swans extract the essence from milk and spit out the water, so should we extract the essence from our lives by practicing discriminating wisdom and engaging in activities that benefit both ourselves and others in this and future lives.

Every sentient being aspires to the highest state of happiness and complete freedom from every kind of suffering, but human aims should be higher than those of animals, insects and so forth because we have much greater potential. With our special intellectual capacity we can accomplish many things. As spiritual practitioners, we should strive for happiness and freedom from misery not just for ourselves alone but for all sentient beings. We have the intelligence and the ability to practice the methods for realizing these goals. We can start from where we are and gradually attain higher levels of being until we attain final perfection. Some people can even attain the highest goal, enlightenment, in a single lifetime.

---

[25] According to Indian legend, swans are able to extract milk from water, that is, take the essence. The quote comes from Atisha's *Entering into the Two Truths*. See Atisha, *The Complete Works of Atisha*, 359, where this verse is translated as

> Life is short and many the kinds of knowledge;
> Let him who knows not even his own life's span,
> Choose only from his purest desires,
> As the goose strains milk from water.

In *A Guide to the Bodhisattva's Way of Life*, the great yogi and bodhisattva Shantideva wrote,

> Although we want all happiness,
> We ignorantly destroy it, like an enemy.
> Although we want no misery,
> We rush to create its cause.[26]

What we want and what we do are totally contradictory. The things we do to bring happiness actually cause suffering, misery and trouble. Shantideva says that even though we desire happiness, out of ignorance we destroy its cause as if it were our worst enemy.

According to the Buddha's teachings, first we must learn, or study. By asking if it's possible to escape from suffering and find perfect happiness, we open the doors of spiritual inquiry and discover that by putting our effort and wisdom in the right direction, we can indeed experience such goals. This leads us to seek out the path to enlightenment. The Buddha set forth many different levels of teachings. As humans, we can learn these, not just for the sake of learning but in order to put the methods into practice.

THE REAL ENEMY

What is the cause of happiness? What is the cause of misery? These are important questions in Buddhism. The Buddha pointed out that the fundamental source of all our problems is the wrong conception of the self. We always hold on to some kind of I, some sort of egocentric thought or attitude, and everything we do is based on this wrong conception of the nature of the self. This self-grasping gives rise to attachment to the I and self-centeredness, the cherishing of ourselves over all others, all worldly thoughts and samsara itself. All sentient beings' problems start here.

[26] Chapter 1, verse 28.

This ignorant self-grasping creates all of our attachment to the I. From "me" comes "mine"—*my* property, *my* body, *my* mind, *my* family, *my* friends, *my* house, *my* country, *my* work and so forth.

From attachment come aversion, anger and hatred for the things that threaten our objects of attachment. Buddhism calls these three—ignorance, attachment and aversion—the three poisons. These delusions are the cause of all our problems. They are our real enemies.

We usually look for enemies outside, but Buddhist yogis realize that there are no external enemies; the real enemies are within. Once we have removed ignorance, attachment and aversion we have vanquished our inner enemies. Correct understanding replaces ignorance, pure mind remains, and we see the true nature of the self and all phenomena. The workings of the illusory world no longer occur.

When ignorance has gone, we no longer create mistaken actions. When we act without mistake, we no longer experience the various sufferings—the forces of karma are not engaged. Karma—the actions of the body, speech and mind of sentient beings, together with the seeds they leave on the mind—is brought under control. Since the causes of these actions—ignorance, attachment and aversion—have been destroyed, the actions to which they give rise therefore cease.

Ignorance, attachment and aversion, together with their branches of conceit, jealousy, envy and so forth, are very strong forces. Once they arise, they immediately dominate our mind; we quickly fall under the power of these inner enemies and no longer have any freedom or control. Our inner enemies even cause us to fight with and harm the people we love; they can even cause us to kill our own parents, children and so forth. All conflicts—from those between individual members of a family to international wars between countries—arise from these negative thoughts.

Shantideva said, "There is one cause of all problems." This is the ignorance that mistakes the actual nature of the self. All sentient beings are similar in that they are all overpowered by this ego-grasping ignorance; however, each of us is also capable of engaging in the yogic practices that refine the mind to the point where it is able to see directly the way things exist.

How the Buddha practiced and taught Dharma

Buddha himself first studied, then practiced, and finally realized Dharma, achieving enlightenment. He saw the principles of the causes and effects of thought and action and then taught people how to work with these laws in such a way as to gain freedom.

His first teaching was on the four truths as seen by a liberated being: suffering, its cause, liberation and the path to liberation.[27] First we must learn to recognize the sufferings and frustrations that pervade our lives. Then we must know their cause. Thirdly we should know that it is possible to get rid of them, to be completely free. Lastly we must know the truth of the path—the means by which we can gain freedom—the methods of practice that destroy the seeds of suffering from their very root.

There are many elaborate ways of presenting the path, which has led to the development of many schools of Buddhism, such as the Hinayana and Mahayana, but the teachings of the four truths are fundamental to all Buddhist schools; each has its own special methods, but all are based on the four truths. Without the four truths there is neither Hinayana nor Mahayana. All Buddhist schools see suffering as the main problem of existence and ignorance as the main cause of suffering. Without removing ignorance there is no way to achieve liberation from samsara and no way to attain the perfect enlightenment of buddhahood.

---

[27] As detailed by the Dalai Lama in the previous chapter.

UTILIZING THE FOUR TRUTHS

Buddhism talks a lot about non-self or the empty nature of all things. This is a key teaching. The realization of emptiness was first taught by the Buddha and then widely disseminated by the great teacher Nagarjuna and his successors, who explained the philosophy of the Middle Way—a system of thought free from all extremes. Madhyamikas, as the followers of this system are called, hold that the way things actually exist is free from the extremes of ultimate being and non-being. The things we see do not exist in the way that we perceive them.

As for the I, our understanding of its nature is also mistaken. This doesn't mean that there is neither person nor desire. When the Buddha rejected the existence of a self he meant that the self *we normally conceive* does not exist. Yogis who, through meditation, have developed higher insight have realized the true nature of the self and seen that the I exists totally in another way. They have realized the emptiness of the self, which is the key teaching of the Buddha; they have developed the sharp weapon of wisdom that cuts down the poisonous tree of delusion and mental distortion.

To do the same, we must study the teachings, contemplate them carefully and finally investigate our conclusions through meditation. In that way we can realize the true nature of the self. The wisdom realizing emptiness cuts the very root of all delusion and puts an end to all suffering; it directly opposes the ignorance that misconceives reality.

Sometimes we can apply more specific antidotes—for example, when anger arises we meditate on compassion; when lust arises we meditate on the impurity of the human body; when attachment to situations arises we meditate on impermanence; and so forth. But even though these antidotes counteract particular delusions they cannot cut their root—for that, we need to realize emptiness.

Combining wisdom and method

However, wisdom alone is not enough. No matter how sharp an axe is, it requires a handle and a person to swing it. In the same way, while meditation on emptiness is the key practice, it must be supported and given direction by method. Many Indian masters, including Dharmakirti and Shantideva, have asserted this to be so. For example, meditation upon the four noble truths includes contemplation of sixteen aspects of these truths, such as impermanence, suffering, and so forth. Then, because we must share our world with others there are the meditations on love, compassion and bodhicitta, the enlightened attitude of wishing for enlightenment in order to be of greatest benefit to others. This introduces the six perfections, or the means of accomplishing enlightenment—generosity, discipline, patience, energy, meditation and wisdom. The first five of these must act as supportive methods in order for the sixth, wisdom, to become stable.

Removing the obstacles to liberation and omniscience

If we are to attain buddhahood, we must completely remove the obstacles to it. These obstacles are of two main types: obstacles to liberation, which include delusions such as attachment, and obstacles to omniscience. When we have removed the various delusions, we become an arhat. In Tibetan, arhat (*dra-chom-pa*) means one who has destroyed (*chom*) the inner enemy (*dra*) and has thus gained liberation from all delusions. However, liberation is not buddhahood.

An arhat is free from samsara, from all misery and suffering, and no longer forced to take a rebirth conditioned by karma and delusion. At present we are strongly under the power of these two forces, being reborn again and again, sometimes higher, sometimes lower. We have little choice or independence in our birth, life, death and rebirth. Negative karma and delusion combine and overpower us again and again. Our freedom is thus greatly limited. It is a circle: occasionally we're reborn in a high realm, then in a lower one; sometimes a human or a god, sometimes an animal. This is what samsara means. Arhats have achieved complete liberation from this circle; they have broken the circle and gone beyond it. Their lives have become totally pure, totally free. The forces that controlled them have gone and they dwell in a state of emancipation from compulsive experience. Their realization of emptiness is complete.

On the method side, the arhat has cultivated a path combining meditation on emptiness with meditation on the impermanence of life, karma and its results, the suffering nature of the whole circle of samsara and so forth, but arhatship does not have the perfection of buddhahood.

Compared to our ordinary samsaric life, arhatship is a great attainment, but arhats still have subtle obstacles. Gross mental obstacles such as desire, hatred, ignorance and so forth may have gone but, because they have been active forces within the mind for so long, they leave behind subtle hindrances—subtle habits, or predispositions.

For example, although arhats will not have anger, old habits, such as using harsh words, may persist. They also have a very subtle self-centeredness. Similarly, although arhats do not have ignorance or wrong views, they cannot see certain aspects of cause and effect as clearly as a buddha can. Such subtle limitations are called the obstacles to omniscience. In buddhahood, these have been completely removed; not a single obstacle remains. There is both perfect freedom and perfect knowledge.

THE WISDOM AND FORM BODIES OF A BUDDHA

A buddha has a cause. The cause is a bodhisattva. The bodhisattva trainings are vast: generosity, where we try to help others in various ways; patience, which keeps our mind in a state of calm; enthusiastic perseverance, with which we joyfully undergo many hardships without hesitation in order to help other sentient beings; and many others.

Before attaining buddhahood we have to train as a bodhisattva and cultivate a path uniting method with wisdom. The function of wisdom is to eliminate ignorance; the function of method is to produce the physical and environmental perfections of being.

Buddhahood is endowed with many qualities—perfect body and mind, omniscient knowledge, power and so forth—and from the perfection of the inner qualities, a buddha manifests a perfect environment, a "pure land."

With the ripening of wisdom and method comes the fruit: the wisdom and form bodies of a buddha. The form body, or rupakaya, has two aspects—*sambhogakaya* and *nirmanakaya*—which, with the wisdom body of dharmakaya, constitute the three kayas. The form bodies are not ordinary form; they are purely mental, a reflection or manifestation of the dharmakaya wisdom. From perfect wisdom emerges perfect form.

CHERISHING OTHERS

As we can see from the above examples, the bodhisattva's activities are based on a motivation very unlike our ordinary attitudes, which are usually selfish and self-centered. In order to attain buddhahood we have to change our mundane thoughts into thoughts of love and compassion for other sentient beings. We have to learn to care, all of the time, on a universal level. Our normal self-centered attitude should be seen as an enemy and a loving and compassionate attitude as the cause of the highest happiness, a real friend of both ourselves and others.

The Mahayana contains a very special practice called "exchanging self for others." Of course, I can't change into you and you can't change into me; that's not what it means. What we have to change is the attitude of "me first" into the thought of cherishing of others: "Whatever bad things have to happen let them happen to me." Through meditation we learn to regard self-centeredness as our worst enemy and to transform self-cherishing into love and compassion until eventually our entire life is dominated by these positive forces. Then everything we do becomes beneficial for others; all our actions naturally become meritorious. This is the influence and power of the bodhisattva's thought—the bodhi mind, the ultimate flowering of love and compassion into the determination to attain enlightenment for the benefit of all other sentient beings.

LOVE AND COMPASSION

Love and compassion have the same basic nature but a different referent, or application. Compassion is mainly in reference to the problems of beings, the wish to free sentient beings from suffering, whereas love refers to the positive side, the aspiration that all sentient beings have happiness and its cause. Our love and compassion should be equal toward all beings and have the intensity that a loving mother feels toward her only child, taking upon ourselves full responsibility for the well-being of others. That's how bodhisattvas regard all sentient beings.

However, the bodhi mind is not merely love and compassion. Bodhisattvas see that in order to free sentient beings from misery and give them the highest happiness, they themselves have to be fully equipped, fully qualified—first they have to attain perfect buddhahood, total freedom from all obstacles and limitations and complete possession of all power and knowledge. Right now we can't do much to benefit others. Therefore, for the benefit of other sentient beings, we have to attain enlightenment as quickly as possible. Day and night, everything we do should be done in order to reach perfect enlightenment as soon as we can for the benefit of others.

BODHICITTA

The thought characterized by this aspiration is called bodhicitta, bodhi mind, the bodhisattva spirit. Unlike our usual self-centered, egotistical thoughts, which lead only to desire, hatred, jealousy, pride and so forth, the bodhisattva way is dominated by love, compassion and the bodhi mind, and if we practice the appropriate meditative techniques, we ourselves will become bodhisattvas. Then, as Shantideva has said, all our ordinary activities—sleeping, walking, eating or whatever—will naturally produce limitless goodness and fulfill the purposes of many sentient beings.

THE LIFE OF A BODHISATTVA

A bodhisattva's life is very precious and therefore, in order to sustain it, we sleep, eat and do whatever else is necessary to stay alive. Because this is our motivation for eating, every mouthful of food we take gives rise to great merit, equal to the number of the sentient beings in the universe.

In order to ascend the ten bodhisattva stages leading to buddhahood, we engage in both method and wisdom—on the basis of bodhicitta we cultivate the realization of emptiness. Seeing the emptiness of the self, our self-grasping ignorance and attachment cease. We also see all phenomena as empty and, as a result, everything that appears to our mind is seen as illusory, like a magician's creations.

When a magician conjures something up, people in the audience believe that what they see exists. However, although the magician sees what the audience sees, he understands it differently. When he creates a beautiful woman, men in the audience may experience lust; when he creates a frightening animal, the audience may get scared. The magician sees the beautiful woman and the scary animal just as the audience does, but he knows that they're not real; he knows that they're empty of existing in the way that they appear, that their reality is not like the mode of their appearance.

Similarly, bodhisattvas who have seen emptiness see everything as illusory, and things that might have caused attachment or aversion to arise before no longer do so.

As Nagarjuna said,

> By combining the twofold cause of method and wisdom, bodhisattvas gain the twofold effect of the mental and physical bodies of a buddha.

Their accumulation of meritorious energy and wisdom bring them to the first bodhisattva stage, where they directly realize emptiness and overcome the obstacles to liberation. They then use this realization to progress through the ten bodhisattva levels, eventually eradicating all obstacles to omniscience. They first eliminate the coarse level of ignorance and then, through gradual meditation on method combined with wisdom, attain the perfection of enlightenment.

THE KEYS TO THE MAHAYANA PATH

The main subjects of this discourse—renunciation, emptiness and the bodhi mind—were taught by the Buddha, Nagarjuna and Tsongkhapa and provide the basic texture of the Mahayana path. These three principal aspects of the path are like keys for those who want to attain enlightenment. In terms of method and wisdom, renunciation and the bodhi mind constitute method, and meditation on emptiness is wisdom. Method and wisdom are like the two wings of a bird and enable us to fly high in the sky of Dharma. Just as a bird with one wing cannot fly, in order to reach the heights of buddhahood we need the two wings of method and wisdom.

RENUNCIATION

The principal Mahayana method is the bodhi mind. To generate the bodhi mind we must first generate compassion—the aspiration to free sentient beings from suffering, which becomes the basis of our motivation to attain enlightenment. However, as Shantideva pointed out, we must begin with compassion for ourselves. We must want to be free of suffering ourselves before being truly able to want it for others. The spontaneous wish to free ourselves from suffering is renunciation.

But most of us don't have it. We don't see the faults of samsara. However, there's no way to really work for the benefit of others while continuing to be entranced by the pleasures and activities of samsara. Therefore, first we have to generate personal renunciation of samsara—the constant wish to gain freedom from all misery. At the beginning, this is most important. Then we can extend this quality to others as love, compassion and the bodhi mind, which combine as method. When united with the wisdom realizing emptiness, we possess the main causes of buddhahood.

MAKING THIS LIFE MEANINGFUL

Of course, to develop the three principal aspects of the path, we have to proceed step by step. Therefore it's necessary to study, contemplate and meditate. We should all try to develop a daily meditation practice. Young or old, male or female, regardless of race, we all have the ability to meditate. Anybody can progress through the stages of understanding. The human life is very meaningful and precious but it can be lost to seeking temporary goals such as sensual indulgence, fame, reputation and so forth, which benefit this life alone. Then we're like animals; we have the goals of the animal world. Even if we don't make heroic spiritual efforts, we should at least try to get started in the practices that make human life meaningful.

Q. Could you clarify what you mean by removing the suffering of others?

Geshe Sopa: We are not talking about temporary problems,

like hunger and thirst. You can do acts of charity with food, medicine and so forth, but these provide only superficial help. Giving can never fulfill the world's needs and can itself become a cause of trouble and misery. What beings lack is perfect happiness and enjoyment. Therefore we cultivate a compassion for all sentient beings that wishes to provide them with the highest happiness, the happiness that lasts forever. Practitioners, yogis and bodhisattvas consider this to be the main goal. They do give temporary things as much as possible, but their main point is to produce a higher happiness. That's the bodhisattva's main function.

Q. Buddhism believes strongly in past and future lives. How is this consistent with the idea of impermanence taught by Buddha?

Geshe Sopa: Because things are impermanent they are changeable. Because impurity is impermanent, purity is possible. Conventional truth can function because of the existence of ultimate truth. Impurity becomes pure; imperfect becomes perfect. Change can cause conditions to switch. By directing our life correctly we can put an end to negative patterns. If things were not impermanent there would be no way to change and evolve.

In terms of karma and rebirth, impermanence means that we can gain control over the stream of our life, which is like a great river, never the same from one moment to the next. If we let polluted tributaries flow into a river it becomes dirty. Similarly, if we let bad thoughts, distorted perceptions and wrong actions control our lives, we evolve negatively and take low rebirths.

If, on the other hand, we control the flow of our life skillfully, we'll evolve positively, take high rebirths and perhaps even attain the highest wisdom of buddhahood. Then the coming and going of imperfect experiences will subside and the impermanent flow of pure perfection will come to us. When that happens we'll have achieved the ultimate human goal.

Q. In the example of the river, its content is flowing water, sometimes muddy, sometimes clear. What is the content of the stream of life?

Geshe Sopa: Buddhism speaks of the five skandhas: one mainly physical, the other four mental. There is also a basis, which is a certain kind of propensity that is neither physical nor mental, a kind of energy. The five impure skandhas eventually become perfectly pure and then manifest as the enlightened beings of the five buddha lineages, or families.

Q. What is the role of prayer in Buddhism? Does Buddhism believe in prayer, and if so, since Buddhists don't believe in a God, to whom do they pray?

Geshe Sopa: In Buddhism, prayer means some kind of wish, an aspiration to have something good occur. In this sense, a prayer is a verbal wish. The prayers of buddhas and bodhisattvas are mental and have great power. Buddhas and bodhisattvas have equal love and compassion for all sentient beings and their prayers are to benefit all sentient beings. Therefore, when we pray to them for help or guidance they have the power to influence us.

As well as these considerations, prayer produces a certain kind of buddha-result. Praying does not mean that personally you don't have to practice yourself; that you just leave everything to the Buddha. It's not like that. The buddhas have to do something and we have to do something. The buddhas cannot wash away our stains with water, like washing clothing. The root of misery and suffering cannot be extracted like a thorn from the foot—the buddhas can only show us how to pull it out; the hand that pulls it out must be our own.

Also, the Buddha cannot transplant his knowledge into our being. He is like a doctor who diagnoses our illnesses and prescribes the cure that we must follow through personal responsibility. If a patient does not take the prescribed medicine or follow the advice, the doctor cannot help, no matter how strong his medicine or excellent his skill. If we take the medicine of Dharma as prescribed and follow the Buddha's advice, we will easily cure ourselves of the diseases of ignorance, attachment and the other obstacles to liberation and omniscience. To turn to the Dharma but then not practice it is to be like a patient burdened by a huge bag of medicine while not taking any. Therefore the Buddha said, "I have provided the medicine. It is up to you to take it."

Q. Sometimes in meditation we visualize Shakyamuni Buddha. What did he visualize when he meditated?

Geshe Sopa: What should we meditate upon? How should we meditate? Shakyamuni Buddha himself meditated in the same way as we teach: on compassion, love, bodhicitta, the four noble truths and so forth. Sometimes he also meditated on perfect forms, like that of a buddha or a particular meditational deity. These deities symbolize perfect inner qualities and through meditating on them we bring ourselves into proximity with the symbolized qualities. Both deity meditation and ordinary simple meditations tame the scattered, uncontrolled, elephant-like mind. The wild, roaming mind must be calmed in order to enter higher spiritual practices. Therefore, at the beginning, we try to stabilize our mind by focusing it on a particular subject. This is calm abiding meditation and its main aim is to keep our mind focused on a single point, abiding in perfect clarity and peace for as long as we wish without any effort, wavering or fatigue.

As for the object to be visualized in this type of meditation, there are many choices: a candle, a statue, an abstract object and so forth. Since the form of an enlightened being has many symbolic values and shares the nature of the goal we hope to accomplish, visualizing such an object has many advantages. But it is not mandatory; we can choose anything. The main thing is to focus the mind on the object and not allow it to waver. Eventually we'll be able to meditate clearly and peacefully for as long as we like, remaining absorbed for even days at a time. This is the attainment of calm abiding. When we possess this mental instrument, every other meditation we do will become much more successful.

When we first try this kind of practice we discover that our mind is like a wild elephant, constantly running here and there, never able to focus fully on or totally engage in anything. Then, little by little, through practice and exercise, it will become calm, and even concentrating on a simple object like breathing in and out while counting will demonstrate the wildness of the mind and the calming effects of meditation.

Geshe Lhundub Sopa (1923–2014) was a great scholar from Sera Monastery renowned for his insight into emptiness and one of His Holiness the Dalai Lama's debate examiners in Tibet, 1959, just before fleeing the Chinese occupation for India. He came to the USA in 1962 and joined the faculty of the University of Madison, Wisconsin, in 1967, where he remained until his retirement in 1997. He was the spiritual head of Deer Park Buddhist Center, Wisconsin. He is the author of *Steps on the Path to Enlightenment*, a comprehensive commentary on Lama Tsongkhapa's *Lam-rim Chen-mo*. His autobiography, *Like a Waking Dream*, was published in 2012. Geshe Rinpoche gave this teaching at Tushita Mahayana Meditation Centre, New Delhi, 30 July 1980. It was first published in *Teachings at Tushita* in 1981.

RENUNCIATION

Tsenshab Serkong Rinpoche

BRIAN BERESFORD

DHARMA PROTECTS US FROM SUFFERING

THE SANSKRIT WORD *Dharma* means to hold, or uphold. What is it that Dharma upholds, or maintains? It is the elimination of suffering and the attainment of happiness. Dharma does this not only for us but for all other sentient beings as well.

The sufferings we experience are of two types: those immediately visible to us as humans and those we cannot see without psychic powers. The former include the pain involved in the birth process, the unpleasantness of occasionally becoming sick, the misery experienced by growing old and aging, and the terror of death.

The sufferings that come after death are not visible to an ordinary person. We might think that when we die we will probably be reborn as a human being. However, this is not necessarily the case. There is no logical reason for us to assume that such an evolution will occur. Nor is it the case that after we die we will not take rebirth at all.

As for the particular type of rebirth we will take, this is very difficult to predict; it's not within our present sphere of knowledge. If we generate positive karma during this life, it will naturally follow that we will take happy forms of rebirth in the future. Conversely, if we create mostly negative karma, we will not take a happy rebirth but experience great difficulties in lower states of being. This is certain. That's the way rebirth works. If you plant a wheat seed, a wheat plant grows; if you plant a rice seed, a rice plant is produced. Similarly, if you create negative karma, you're planting the seeds of rebirth in one of the three lower states as a hell being, a hungry ghost or an animal.

Although the sufferings of the hell beings and hungry ghosts may be invisible to us, we can see those of the animals with our own eyes. If we wonder what it would be like if we ourselves were to be reborn as animals, we can just look at those around us and imagine what it would be like to be in their condition. Dharma is that which holds us back and protects us from experiencing the suffering of the three lower realms.

However, the entire wheel of rebirth, the whole of cyclic existence, is in the nature of suffering. Dharma safeguards us from all of it. Moreover, Mahayana Dharma, the teachings of the Great Vehicle, protects not only us but also all other living beings.

In Buddhism, we hear a lot about the Three Jewels of Refuge—Buddha, Dharma and Sangha. The first of these includes all the fully enlightened beings who teach the Dharma. For us, Buddha Shakyamuni, who first turned the wheel of Dharma at Sarnath by teaching the four noble truths, is the most significant. The last of these four truths—the truth of the path—is the Dharma that we must practice in order to achieve liberation. This is the refuge object called the Dharma jewel.

THE CAUSE OF SUFFERING

Dharma practice entails two things: recognizing and eradicating the root of samsaric suffering. What is the root of cyclic existence? It is the grasping at a truly existent self and at truly existent phenomena. Therefore, we need to develop revulsion for this grasping that brings us all our suffering and an understanding of the antidote to it. The antidote to grasping at true existence is the wisdom realizing selflessness; a deep understanding of selflessness will liberate us from suffering.

The sufferings we experience in cyclic existence are caused by the karma created by our acting under the influence of the delusions. When we understand this, we aspire to obtain the antidote to self-grasping. Why have we not yet developed this antidote in our mindstream; why don't we understand selflessness? One reason is that we are not sufficiently aware of impermanence and death.

CONTEMPLATING IMPERMANENCE AND DEATH

The only possible outcome of birth is death. We are inevitably going to die. There has never been a sentient being whose life did not end with death. People try many methods to prevent death from occurring, but it's impossible. No medicine can cure us of death.

But just thinking "I'm going to die" isn't really the correct way to contemplate death. Of course, everybody is going to die, but merely recalling this fact is not very powerful. It is not the proper method. Similarly, just thinking of the fact that our body is constantly disintegrating and deteriorating and will eventually fail is also not enough. What we have to think about is how to prevent all this from happening.

If we think about the fear that we'll experience at the time of death and how to eliminate it, our meditation on death will be effective. People who have accumulated much negative karma during their lives become very frightened at the time of death. They cry, drool, excrete into their clothing and are completely overwhelmed—clear signs of the fear and suffering that occur at death because of negative actions created during life.

Alternatively, if during our lifetime we refrain from committing negative actions, death will be very easy to face. Death can be a joyous experience, like that of a child coming home. If we have purified ourselves, we can die happily. By abstaining from the ten nonvirtuous actions and cultivating their opposites, the ten virtues, our death will be easy and, as a result, we won't have to experience rebirth in conditions of suffering. We will be assured of rebirth in more fortunate states.

If we plant seeds of medicinal plants, we get trees with medicinal powers; if we plant seeds of poisonous trees, we get poisonous fruit. Similarly, if we plant the seeds of virtuous actions on our consciousness, we will experience happiness in future rebirths; we will experience good fortune, both mentally and physically. This basic Dharma teaching of avoiding the ten nonvirtuous deeds and cultivating the ten virtues is given not only in Buddhism but also in many other religions.

If simply thinking "I'm going to die" is not very beneficial, how then should we contemplate death and impermanence? We should think, "If I have created any of the ten nonvirtuous actions, when I die I will have to face great fear and suffering and will be reborn into unimaginable misery. If, on the other hand, I have created virtue, when I die I will not experience much fear or suffering and will be reborn into a fortunate state." That is the correct way to think about death.

This meditation is not thinking gloomily and pessimistically, "I'm going to die and there's nothing I can do about it," but rather contemplating intelligently, "Where will I go after death? What sort of causes have I created? Can I make my death a happy one? How? Can I make my future rebirths happy? How?"

When contemplating future rebirths we should remember that there is no place in cyclic existence that is reliable. No matter what body we obtain, it must eventually pass away. We read accounts of people who have lived for a hundred or even a thousand years, but no matter how fantastic their stories, they have all had to die. All samsaric bodies are subject to death.

Moreover, there is no place to which we can run to escape death. No matter where we are, when the time comes, we'll have to die. At that time, no amount of medicine, mantra or practice will help. Surgery can cure certain diseases but it can't prevent death.

Also, no matter what type of rebirth we gain, it too will be subject to death. The process is ongoing. Contemplating the long-range effects of our actions and the continuity of the process of birth, life, death and rebirth will help us generate much positive karma.

Even though we sometimes plan to practice Dharma, we usually plan to do so tomorrow or the day after. However, we can't tell when we're going to die. If we were guaranteed a hundred years to live we'd be able to plan our practice long-range, but we have not the slightest certainty of when we're going to die. Therefore, it's very foolish to put our practice off. Some people die in the womb before they're even born; others die as small babies before they've even learned to walk. There's no logic in thinking that we're going to live long.

Furthermore, our body is very fragile. If it were made of stone or iron we could be excused for thinking that it was very stable, but we can easily see that it's extremely weak and liable to go wrong at any moment. It's like a delicate wristwatch made of countless tiny, fragile parts. Our body is not to be trusted. And there are many circumstances that can cause our death: food that has become poisonous, the bite of a small insect or the prick of a tiny thorn. Such seemingly insignificant conditions can kill us. Even the food and drink we ingest to extend our life can become the circumstances that end it. There's no certainty as to when we'll die or what will cause our death.

Even if we feel certain that we'll live a hundred years, many of those years have already passed and we haven't accomplished much. We approach death like somebody asleep in a railway carriage, constantly getting closer and closer to the destination but unaware of the process. Of course, there's nothing we can do to stop it. We just constantly get ever closer to death.

No matter how much money, jewelry, houses or clothes we accumulate in life, it makes no difference whatsoever at the time of death. When we die, we go to the next life empty-handed; we cannot take even the tiniest material object with us. Even our body must be left behind; our mind and body separate and our mind goes on alone.

If at death we have to leave our body, our friends and all our possessions, what, then, accompanies our consciousness at that time? Is there anything that can go with it to the next life? Yes, there is. When we die, the karmic imprints that we have accumulated during our life accompany our consciousness.

CREATING POSITIVE AND NEGATIVE KARMA

If we have created any of the ten nonvirtuous actions, a negative karmic debt accompanies our mindstream as it evolves into the future rebirth. By killing other beings, stealing others' possessions or indulging in sexual misconduct, we leave karmic imprints of these negative physical actions on our consciousness. By lying, slandering other people and causing disunity among them, gossiping or speaking harshly, harming others with words, we leave karmic imprints of these negative verbal actions on our consciousness. By harboring covetous thoughts, wishing to have the possessions of others; generating ill will toward others, wishing them harm; or holding distorted views, such as "there are no past or future lives," "there's no such thing as cause and effect" or "there's no such thing as refuge," we leave karmic imprints of these negative mental actions on our consciousness. All these negative karmic debts travel with and direct our mind into future rebirths.

The reverse is also true. If we turn away from negativity and create virtuous actions of body, speech and mind, the karmic seeds of these positive actions also travel on our mind-stream and produce better circumstances in our future lives.

If we really think about the situation we're in we'll resolve to try to generate positive karma and eliminate its opposite in whatever way we can. In other words, we should try to create as little negativity as possible and purify the seeds of past negative actions so that not even the smallest karmic debt remains to be repaid in our future lives.

We also need to look at the kinds of result that can happen within the law of cause and effect. For example, there's the story of a person who had many good qualities but was harsh in his speech. Once he abused another person by saying, "You talk like a dog." As a result, he himself was reborn as a dog five hundred times. Seemingly small negative actions can bring devastating effects.

Similarly, however, small positive actions can also produce great results. For example, there's the story of the young child who made a humble offering to the Buddha and as a result was reborn as the great king Ashoka, who built thousands of stupas and performed countless other sublime activities.

DEVELOPING RENUNCIATION

Contemplating the various nonvirtues we have committed and their results is a very effective way of ensuring our welfare and happiness. When we think of the suffering we ourselves will have to bear as a result of our negativities, we'll give birth to the strong, indestructible wish not to have to experience all this misery and will have developed what is called renunciation.

Acquainting ourselves with this type of thinking is itself a form of meditation—analytical meditation. First we develop mindfulness of our own suffering; then we extend this mindfulness to the suffering of all other sentient beings. Considering deeply how all beings want to be completely free of all suffering but are caught in a net of suffering from which they cannot escape leads to compassion.

If we don't develop the wish to be free from all our own suffering, how can we develop the wish for others to be free from theirs? We can put an end to our own suffering, but this in itself is not ultimately beneficial. We need to extend this wish to all living beings, who also desire happiness. We can train our mind to develop the wish for all sentient beings to be completely parted from their sufferings. This is a much wider and more beneficial way of thinking.

Why should we concern ourselves with the suffering of other living beings? It's because we receive so much from others: the milk we drink comes from the kindness of others, the warm clothing that protects us from the wind and cold, the house we live in, the money we receive, our precious human body—all these things come from the kindness of others; the list is endless. However, just these few examples should be enough to show us why we should try to find a method that can eliminate the suffering of all the kind mother sentient beings.

No matter what kind of practice we do—the recitation of mantras, any other kind of meditation, whatever it is—we should always do it with the thought, "May this benefit all living beings." Not only will this help others; it will naturally benefit us as well. Ordinary life situations can give us an appreciation of this: somebody who is very selfish and always works for his or her own gain is never really liked by others whereas somebody who is very kind and always helping others is usually very popular.

The thought we must develop in our mindstream is, "May all beings be happy and may none of them suffer." We should try to incorporate this thought into our own thinking by remembering it again and again. This will be extremely beneficial. Those who in the past developed this thought are now great buddhas, bodhisattvas or saints; all the truly great people of the world based their lives upon it. How wonderful it would be if we could try to generate this thought within ourselves.

Q. Are we advised not to defend ourselves when somebody tries to harm us?

Serkong Rinpoche. That question introduces a very extensive subject. If somebody hits you over the head with a stick, the best response is to meditate that you experienced this because of your own past negative actions. Think how this person is allowing that particular karmic debt to ripen now rather than at some future time. You should feel gratitude that this person has eliminated that negative karmic debt from your mindstream.

Q. What if somebody attacks my wife or child, who are under my protection? Should I not defend them? Would it be negative to do so?

Serkong Rinpoche. As it is your duty to protect your wife and child, you must try to do so as skillfully as possible. You have to be clever. The best way to protect them is without harming their attacker. In other words, you have to find a method of protecting them whereby you do not inflict any harm.

Q. He can he harm my children but I cannot harm him? Is it not our duty to defend our children against barbarous and cruel acts? Should we just lay down our lives?

Serkong Rinpoche. In order to handle this situation skillfully you need a great deal of courage. There's a story about a previous life of the Buddha in which he was a navigator who went to sea with a group of five hundred people in search of buried treasure. One of these people had very greedy thoughts of murdering all the others and stealing the jewels for himself. The bodhisattva navigator became aware of the man's intentions and thought it incorrect to let a situation develop where one man killed five hundred. Therefore, he developed the courageous thought of saving the five hundred by killing this one man, willingly accepting upon himself the full responsibility of killing. If you are willing to be reborn in hell in order to save others, you have a greatly courageous thought and can engage in these acts, just as the Buddha himself did.

Q. Under such circumstances, is killing still considered to be a negative action?

Serkong Rinpoche. Nagarjuna says in his *Friendly Letter* that if one commits negativity in the name of protecting one's parents, children, Buddhism or the Three Jewels of Refuge, one will have to experience the consequences. The difference is in whether or not you are aware of the consequences and willing to take them upon yourself in order to selflessly protect your wife and child. If you harm an enemy, you are going to experience a suffering rebirth. However, you should be willing to face this by thinking, "I will take that suffering on myself so that my wife and child don't suffer."

Q. Then according to Buddhism it would still be a nonvirtuous act?

Serkong Rinpoche. Protecting your wife and child is virtuous but harming your enemy is not. You have to be willing to accept the consequences of both actions.

Q. You said that those who create negative karma will suffer in the future but those who do good will experience happiness. Can these good actions lead to complete liberation, in the sense of not having to experience rebirth?

Serkong Rinpoche. If you want to gain complete liberation from cyclic existence, you have to follow the teachings of the Buddha completely and precisely. If you do so correctly, liberation from cyclic existence is definitely possible.

Tsenshab Serkong Rinpoche (1914–83) was born in southern Tibet. His father was one of Tibet's outstanding masters, Serkong Dorje Chang, and was said to be the incarnation of Marpa the translator. His mother was said to be the incarnation of Marpa's wife Dagmema and Rinpoche to be the incarnation of Marpa's son Darma Dode. In 1959 he was the highest incarnate lama of the Ganden Jangtse Monastery and the only one of His Holiness the Dalai Lama's seven spiritual assistants to escape from Tibet. Renowned as a master of both sutra and tantra, Rinpoche gave this teaching at Tushita Mahayana Meditation Centre, 7 December 1979. It was translated by Alex Berzin and first published in *Teachings at Tushita* in 1981.

THE TWELVE LINKS

Geshe Rabten

UNDERSTANDING LEADS TO RENUNCIATION

DHARMA PRACTICE entails more than just calling yourself a Buddhist or making superficial changes in the way you live your life. It means totally integrating the teachings with your mind.

To integrate the teachings with your mind, you must first prepare yourself by cultivating spiritual stability—pure renunciation—within your stream of being. The Tibetan term for renunciation, *nge-jung*,[28] implies that you must first realize that you are caught in the process of rebirth in samsara, a state of being characterized by a great many sufferings. Therefore, at the beginning of your practice you have to realize the true nature of samsara itself and how you exist in it. You must become acutely aware of the unsatisfactory nature of samsara, the condition in which you find yourself. This is very important.

Once you have recognized the true nature of samsara and become sufficiently disillusioned with it, from the depths of your heart you will generate the spontaneous aspiration to liberate yourself from it. This pure, spontaneous, constant aspiration to be free of samsara is renunciation.

Generally, there are two ways to develop the fully renounced mind. The first is to meditate on the two aspects of samsara: its nature of suffering and the causes of this suffering. The second is to meditate on the twelve links of dependent origination, or arising. Here I will discuss briefly the latter.

There are two main ways of presenting the twelve links: the scriptural way, which explains them in terms of how samsara evolves in general, and the experiential way, which explains them in terms of how they are experienced by an individual over a continuum of

---

[28] Sometimes translated as "definite emergence."

lifetimes. These two systems differ slightly in the way the order of the twelve links is presented. I'm going to explain them the second way: how they are experienced.[29]

IGNORANCE

The first of the twelve links is ignorance, the root of all samsaric suffering. The Sanskrit term *avidya* means not seeing and implies an obscuration of mind. To explain precisely what this ignorance is and how it functions requires a great deal of time and energy, so let's just focus on general principles instead.

For example, when we go to teachings we have the intention, "Today I'm going to go and listen to teachings." Whenever we think like this, we all have a certain conception of our "self," or "I." Buddhism calls this sense of self the ego. Our ego is with us at all times and becomes more obvious on certain occasions, like when we encounter highly favorable circumstances or great difficulties. At such times our sense of self becomes more intense and visible than usual. Each of us is subject to our own conception of I. We can see it quite easily in our daily experiences without need of lengthy, theoretical reasoning.

Whenever our ego-concept arises very strongly, it grasps us as if it exists within us as something very solid, very vivid and totally uncontrollable. This is how the false self grasps us. However, it is important to contemplate whether or not this I really exists as it appears. If we search for it within ourselves, from the top of our head down to the soles of our feet, we'll come to the conclusion that neither our physical body nor any of its individual parts can serve as the I that arises so strongly under certain circumstances. Nothing in our body can be the I. Our limbs, organs and so forth are simply parts of the body, which, in a sense, "owns" them.

[29] See the Dalai Lama, *The Meaning of Life*, for a book-length teaching on the twelve links.

If we analyze our mind in the same way, we'll find that the mind is nothing but a stream of different thoughts and mental factors and conclude that nothing in the mind is the I that we conceive either.

Moreover, since there's no separate entity outside our body or mind to represent the I, we can conclude that the self that we normally feel doesn't exist. If we meditate like this, we'll see that it's true that the I cannot be found. However, this doesn't mean we don't exist at all. Nonexistence cannot be the answer because we're analyzing how we exist.

Actually, the situation is very subtle. We neither exist as simply as the ignorant mind supposes nor do we not exist, and gaining an understanding of the true nature of the self requires thorough training and sustained meditation practice.

The mental factor that holds the wrong, fabricated view of the self is what Buddhism means by ignorance, the first of the twelve links of dependent origination. All the other delusions—such as attachment to ourselves, our friends and possessions and aversion to people and things alien to us—rest on the foundation of this false concept of the self. Acting under the influence of such attachment and aversion, we accumulate much unwholesome karma of body, speech and mind.

VOLITIONAL FORMATIONS

The distorted actions of body, speech and mind that arise from ignorance, attachment and aversion stain the mind with what are called volitional formations. This is the second of the twelve links. The moment after we create a distorted karma, the action itself has passed and is gone, but it leaves on our stream of consciousness an imprint that remains there until it either manifests in the future as a favorable or unfavorable experience, depending on the nature of the original action, or is otherwise disposed of.

CONSCIOUSNESS

The continuity of the mindstream serves as the basis of the imprints of karma. This is the third link, the link of consciousness. It carries the imprints and later helps them ripen and manifest in the same way that seeds are sown in the earth, which then serves as a cause for the growth of a crop. However, not only must seeds be sown in the ground; they also require favorable conditions to grow. Contributory causes such as water, fertilizer and so forth must be present in order for the seeds to ripen and reach maturity.

CRAVING

The attachment that evolves from ignorance helps condition the karmic seeds sown in our stream of consciousness. This particular attachment, which is called craving, is the fourth link.

GRASPING

There also exists in our mindstream another type of attachment, called grasping, which has the special function of bringing karmic seeds to fulfillment. This is the fifth link of the twelve-linked chain. It manifests at the end of our life and conditions the throwing karma that gives rise to our next rebirth.

Although both above types of attachment have the nature of desire, each has its own function. One helps to ripen karmic seeds; the other brings them to completion and connects us with our next life.

BECOMING

The sixth link is becoming. At the end of our life, a throwing karma arises and immediately directs us toward our future existence. This special mental action that appears at the final stage of our life is called "becoming."

These six links are generally associated with this life, although it is not necessarily the case that they will manifest in this life. In particular, some situations may develop in other lifetimes, but in most cases they belong to this life.

As we near death, our body and mind begin to weaken. Bodily strength and the grosser levels of mind dissolve until finally we enter a level of consciousness that the scriptures call the clear light state. This is the final stage of our life, the actual consciousness of death— the subtlest level of mind. We remain in this state for a certain time, then there occurs a slight movement of consciousness and we enter the intermediate state—our mind shoots out of our body and enters the bardo, the realm between death and rebirth.

The intermediate state has its own body and mind, but the body is not made of the same gross elements as ours. Therefore, bardo beings do not have the gross form that we do. The bardo body is composed of a subtle energy called "wind," which exists in a dimension different to ours. We should not think that this is a wonderful or beautiful state, however, for it is characterized by great suffering and difficulty. We undergo a total loss of free will and are driven here and there by the force of karma until we finally find an appropriate place of rebirth. The beings in this state subsist on smell rather than on ordinary food and it is this search for food that eventually leads them to seek rebirth. After a certain period in the bardo state they take rebirth in accordance with their karma.

There are many different realms into which we can take rebirth and each of these has its own causes and conditions. For example, to be born human, our future parents must unite in sexual union,[30] their white and red cells (sperm and ovum) must combine and enter

---

[30] A discussion of how modern developments such as artificial insemination, in vitro fertilization and so forth impact upon this traditional description of conception is beyond the scope of this book.

into the womb of the mother, and so forth. Then, when the bardo being, driven by the force of its individual karma, reaches its karmically determined parents, certain circumstances arise bringing to an end the life of the bardo being, upon which its mind enters the conjoined cells of the parents.

REBIRTH

The moment the wind leaves the bardo body and enters the united cells of the parents, the link of rebirth is established. This is the seventh link. Mere union of the parents, however, is not a sufficient cause for engaging this link. As well, the womb of the mother must be free of obstacles that could interfere with the birth of the child; the material causes of the physical body of the child, that is the parents' sperm and ovum, should also be free from defects; and the three beings involved must have a karmic connection with one another in order to establish this kind of father-mother-child relationship. When all these circumstances are complete, rebirth takes place.

NAME AND FORM

From the time the link of rebirth is established until the sensory organs of the child are developed is the eighth link, which is called name and form. The material substances that constitute the sperm and ovum of the parents are "form"; the consciousness that dwells within that material basis is called "name."

THE SIX SENSE ORGANS

After the sense organs of the child have developed into a mature, functional state, the ninth link, that of the six senses, arises. This is like the construction of a building in which the finishing work, such as windows and doors, has been completed.

CONTACT

The tenth link is contact. After the sense organs have evolved they function through the sense consciousnesses to establish contact with outer sense objects, such as visible forms, sounds and so forth.

FEELING

Contact gives rise to the eleventh link, feeling. Pleasant feelings arise from contact with pleasant objects, unpleasant feelings from unpleasant objects and so forth.

AGING AND DEATH

All this produces the aging process, the twelfth link of the chain of dependent origination, which eventually finishes with our death.

We are all trapped in this process of repeatedly circling on the wheel of birth, aging, death, intermediate state and rebirth. It is not something special that applies to only a few beings or something that happens only to others. It is a process that embraces every one of us. We are caught in cyclic existence and experiencing the twelve links every moment of our existence.

It is very important to contemplate this. If we become fully aware of this constant process of evolution, we'll come to a correct realization of the problems of samsara.

Meditating on this, we'll gradually generate the sincere aspiration to achieve liberation. That aspiration is pure renunciation. However, merely having that aspiration is not enough; we must put great effort into practicing the methods that bring about liberation. On the one hand, we need the help and guidance of the objects of refuge, but from our own side, we must learn and put into practice the actual methods that have been taught. Through the combination of these two, we will attain liberation from the sufferings of samsara.

Geshe Rabten (1921–85) was born in Dhargye in eastern Tibet. He studied at Lhasa's Sera Monastery, where he gained renown as a great scholar, debater and meditation master. In 1959 he escaped to India, where he became the teacher of Lama Yeshe and Lama Zopa Rinpoche. In the mid-60s he was appointed as a spiritual assistant to His Holiness the Dalai Lama. Upon His Holiness's request he began teaching Dharma to Westerners in Dharamsala in 1969 and then went to live and teach in Switzerland in 1974. Geshe Rabten gave this teaching at Tushita Mahayana Meditation Centre 11 April 1980. It was translated by Gonsar Rinpoche and first published in *Teachings at Tushita* in 1981.

The Eight Verses of
Thought Transformation[31]

His Holiness the Dalai Lama

UNKNOWN

[31] See appendix 3 for the root text of *The Eight Verses of Thought Transformation.*

The *Eight Verses of Thought Transformation*, a text by the Kadampa geshe Langri Tangpa, explains the Paramitayana practice of method and wisdom: the first seven verses deal with method—loving kindness, bodhicitta—and the eighth deals with wisdom.[32]

> 1. Determined to obtain the greatest possible benefit from all sentient beings, who are more precious than a wishfulfilling jewel, I shall hold them most dear at all times.

We ourselves and all other beings want to be happy and completely free from suffering. In this we are all exactly equal. However, each of us is only one, while other beings are infinite in number.

Now, there are two attitudes to consider: that of selfishly cherishing ourselves and that of cherishing others. The self-cherishing attitude makes us very uptight; we think we are extremely important and our basic desire is for ourselves to be happy and for things to go well for us. Yet we don't know how to bring this about. In fact, acting out of self-cherishing can never make us happy.

Those who have the attitude of cherishing others regard all other beings as much more important than themselves and value helping others above all else. And, acting in this way, incidentally they themselves become very happy. For example, politicians who are genuinely concerned with helping or serving other people are recorded in history with respect, while those who are constantly exploiting and doing bad things to others go down as examples of bad people.

Leaving aside, for the moment, religion, the next life and nirvana, even within this life selfish people bring negative repercussions

[32] See Lama Zopa Rinpoche's *The Everflowing Nectar of Bodhicitta*, for a complete meditation practice on the *Eight Verses*. FPMT, *Essential Buddhist Prayers, Volume 1*, 155.

down upon themselves by their self-centered actions. On the other hand, people like Mother Teresa, who sincerely devote their entire life and energy to selflessly serving the poor, needy and helpless, are always remembered for their noble work with respect. Others don't have anything negative to say about them. This, then, is the result of cherishing others: whether you want it or not, even those who are not your relatives always like you, feel happy with you and have a warm feeling toward you. If you are the sort of person who always speaks nicely in front of others but complains about them behind their back, of course, nobody will like you.

Thus, even in this life, if we try to help others as much as we can and have as few selfish thoughts as possible, we shall experience much happiness. Our life is not very long; one hundred years at most. If throughout its duration we try to be kind, warm-hearted, concerned for the welfare of others and less selfish and angry, that will be wonderful, excellent; that really is the cause of happiness. If we are selfish, always putting ourselves first and others second, the actual result will be that we ourselves will finish up last. Mentally putting yourself last and others first is the way to come out ahead.

So don't worry about the next life or nirvana; these things will come gradually. If within this life you remain a good, warm-hearted, unselfish person, you will be a good citizen of the world. Whether you are a Buddhist, a Christian or a communist is irrelevant; the important thing is that as long as you are a human being you should be a good human being. That is the teaching of Buddhism; that is the message carried by all the world's religions.

However, the teachings of Buddhism contain every technique for eradicating selfishness and actualizing the attitude of cherishing others. Shantideva's marvelous text, *A Guide to the Bodhisattva's Way of Life*, for example, is very helpful for this. I myself practice according to that book; it is extremely useful. Our mind is very cunning, very difficult to control, but if we make constant effort, work tirelessly with logical reasoning and careful analysis, we shall be able to control it and change it for the better.

Some Western psychologists say that we should not repress our anger but express it—that we should practice anger! However, we must make an important distinction here between mental problems that should be expressed and those that should not. Sometimes you may be truly wronged and it is right for you to express your grievances instead of letting them fester inside you. But you should not express them with anger. If you foster disturbing negative minds such as anger they will become a part of your personality; each time you express anger it becomes easier to express it again. You do it more and more until you are simply a furious person completely out of control. Thus, in terms of mental problems, there are certainly some that are properly expressed but others that are not.

At first when you try to control disturbing negative minds it is difficult. The first day, the first week, the first month you cannot control them well. But with constant effort your negativities will gradually decrease. Progress in mental development does not come about through taking medicines or other chemical substances; it depends on controlling the mind.

Thus we can see that if we want to fulfill our wishes, be they temporal or ultimate, we should rely on other sentient beings much more than on wish-granting gems and always cherish them above all else.

Q. Is the whole purpose of this practice to improve our mind or actually to do something to help others? What is more important?

His Holiness. Both are important. First, if we do not have pure motivation, whatever we do may not be satisfactory. Therefore, the first thing we should do is cultivate pure motivation. But we do not have to wait until that motivation is fully developed before actually doing something to help others. Of course, to help others in the most effective way possible we have to be fully enlightened buddhas. Even to help others in vast and extensive ways we need to have attained one of the levels of a bodhisattva, that is, to have had the experience of a direct, non-conceptual perception of the reality of emptiness and to have achieved the powers of extra-sensory perception. Nonetheless, there are many levels of help we can offer others. Even before we have achieved these qualities we can try to act like bodhisattvas, but naturally our actions will be less effective than theirs. Therefore, without waiting until we are fully qualified, we can generate a good motivation and with that try to help others as best we can. This is a more balanced approach and better than simply staying somewhere in isolation doing some meditation and recitations. Of course, this depends very much on the individual. If we are confident that by staying in a remote place we can gain definite realizations within a certain period, that is different. Perhaps it is best to spend half our time in active work and the other half in the practice of meditation.

Q. Tibet was a Buddhist country. If these values you are describing are Buddhist ones, why was there so much imbalance in Tibetan society.

His Holiness. Human weakness. Although Tibet was certainly a Buddhist country, it had its share of bad, corrupt people. Even some of the religious institutions, the monasteries, became corrupt and turned into centers of exploitation. But all the same, compared with many other societies, Tibet was much more peaceful and harmonious and had fewer problems than they.

> 2. When in the company of others, I shall always consider myself the lowest of all, and from the depths of my heart hold others dear and supreme.

No matter who we are with, we often think things like, "I am stronger than him," "I am more beautiful than her," "I am more intelligent," "I am wealthier," "I am much better qualified" and so forth—we generate much pride. This is not good. Instead, we should always remain humble. Even when we are helping others and are engaged in charity work we should not regard ourselves in a haughty way as great protectors benefiting the weak. This, too, is pride. Rather, we should engage in such activities very humbly and think that we are offering our services up to the people.

When we compare ourselves with animals, for instance, we might think, "I have a human body" or "I'm an ordained person" and feel much higher than them. From one point of view we can say that we have human bodies and are practicing the Buddha's teachings and are thus much better than insects. But from another, we can say that insects are very innocent and free from guile, whereas we often lie and misrepresent ourselves in devious ways in order to achieve our ends or better ourselves. From this point of view we have to say that we are much worse than insects, which just go about their business without pretending to be anything. This is one method of training in humility.

> 3. Vigilant, the moment a delusion appears in my mind,
> endangering myself and others, I shall confront and avert
> it without delay.

If we investigate our mind at times when we are very selfish and preoccupied with ourselves to the exclusion of others, we shall find that the disturbing negative thoughts are the root of this behavior. Since they greatly disturb our mind, the moment we notice that we are coming under their influence we should apply some antidote to them. The general opponent to all the disturbing negative thoughts is meditation on emptiness, but there are also antidotes to specific ones that we, as beginners, can apply. Thus, for attachment, we meditate on ugliness; for anger, on love; for closed-minded ignorance, on dependent arising; for many disturbing thoughts, on the breath and energy winds.

Q. Which dependent arising?
His Holiness. The twelve links of dependent arising. They start

from ignorance and go through to aging and death.[33] On a more subtle level you can use dependent arising as a cause for establishing that things are empty of true existence.

Q. Why should we meditate on ugliness to overcome attachment?

His Holiness. We develop attachment to things because we see them as very attractive. Trying to view them as unattractive, or ugly, counteracts that. For example, we might develop attachment to another person's body, seeing his or her figure as something very attractive. When you start to analyze this attachment you find that it is based on viewing merely the skin. However, the nature of this body that appears to us as beautiful is that of the flesh, blood, bones, skin and so forth of which it is composed. Now let's analyze human skin: take your own, for example. If a piece of it comes off and you put it on your shelf for a few days it becomes really repulsive. This is the nature of skin. All parts of the body are the same. There is no beauty in a piece of human flesh; when you see blood you might feel afraid, not attached. Even a beautiful face: if it gets scratched there is nothing nice about it; wash off the paint—there is nothing left! Ugliness is the nature of the physical body. Human bones, the skeleton, are also repulsive; a skull and crossbones has a very negative connotation.

So that is the way to analyze something toward which you feel attachment, or love—using this word in the negative sense of desirous attachment. Think more of the object's ugly side; analyze the nature of the person or thing from that point of view. Even if this does not control your attachment completely, at least it will help subdue it a little. This is the purpose of meditating on or building up the habit of looking at the ugly aspect of things.

The other kind of love, or kindness, is not based on the reasoning that "such and such a person is beautiful, therefore, I shall show

[33] See Geshe Rabten's teaching on the twelve links, p. 137.

respect and kindness." The basis for pure love is, "This is a living being that wants happiness, does not want suffering and has the right to be happy. Therefore, I should feel love and compassion." This kind of love is entirely different from the first, which is based on ignorance and therefore totally unsound. The reasons for loving-kindness are sound. With the love that is simply attachment, the slightest change in the object, such as a tiny change of attitude, immediately causes you to change. This is because your emotion is based on something very superficial. Take, for example, a new marriage. Often after a few weeks, months or years the couple become enemies and finish up getting divorced. They married deeply in love—nobody chooses to marry with hatred—but after a short time everything changed. Why? Because of the superficial basis of the relationship; a small change in one person causes a complete change of attitude in the other.

We should think, "The other person is a human being like me. Certainly I want happiness; therefore, she must want happiness, too. As a sentient being I have the right to happiness; for the same reason she, too, has the right to happiness." This kind of sound reasoning gives rise to pure love and compassion. Then no matter how our view of that person changes—from good to bad to ugly—she is basically the same sentient being. Thus, since the main reason for showing loving-kindness is always there, our feelings toward the other are perfectly stable.

The antidote to anger is meditation on love, because anger is a very rough, coarse mind that needs to be softened with love.

When we enjoy the objects to which we are attached, we do experience a certain pleasure but, as Nagarjuna has said, it is like having an itch and scratching it—it gives us some pleasure but we would be far better off if we did not have the itch in the first place.[34] Similarly,

---

[34] See Nagarjuna, *Buddhist Advice for Living and Liberation*, verse 169.

> There is pleasure when a sore is scratched,
> But to be without sores is more pleasurable still;
> Just so, there are pleasures in worldly desires,
> But to be without desires is more pleasurable still.

when we get the things with which we are obsessed we feel happy, but we'd be far better off if we were free from the attachment that causes us to become obsessed with things.

> 4. Whenever I see beings that are wicked in nature[35] and overwhelmed by violent negative actions and suffering, I shall hold such rare ones dear, as if I had found a precious treasure.

If we run into somebody who is by nature very cruel, rough, nasty and unpleasant, our usual reaction is to avoid him. In such situations our loving concern for others is liable to decrease. Instead of allowing our love for others to weaken by thinking what an evil person he is, we should see him as a special object of love and compassion and cherish that person as though we had come across a precious treasure, difficult to find.

> 5. When, out of envy, others mistreat me with abuse, insults or the like, I shall accept defeat and offer the victory to others.

If somebody insults, abuses or criticizes us, saying that we are incompetent and don't know how to do anything and so forth, we are likely to get very angry and contradict what the person has said. We should not react in this way; instead, with humility and tolerance, we should accept what has been said.

Where it says that we should accept defeat and offer the victory to others, we have to differentiate two kinds of situation. If, on the one hand, we are obsessed with our own welfare and very selfishly motivated, we should accept defeat and offer victory to the other, even if our life is at stake. But if, on the other hand, the situation

---

[35] This does not mean that these beings' fundamental nature is unchangeably evil but refers more to their character or behavior.

is such that the welfare of others is at stake, we have to work very hard to fight for the rights of others and not accept the loss at all.

One of the forty-six secondary vows of a bodhisattva refers to a situation in which somebody is doing something very harmful and you have to use forceful methods or whatever else is necessary to stop that person's actions immediately—if you don't, you have transgressed that commitment.[36] It might appear that this bodhisattva vow and the fifth stanza, which says that one must accept defeat and give the victory to the other, are contradictory but they are not. The bodhisattva precept deals with a situation in which one's prime concern is the welfare of others: if somebody is doing something extremely harmful and dangerous it is wrong not to take strong measures to stop it if necessary.

Nowadays, in very competitive societies, strong defensive or similar actions are often required. The motivation for these should not be selfish concern but extensive feelings of kindness and compassion toward others. If we act out of such feelings to save others from creating negative karma this is entirely correct.

Q. It may sometimes be necessary to take strong action when we see something wrong, but whose judgment do we trust for such decisions? Can we rely on our own perception of the world?

His Holiness. That's complicated. When you consider taking the loss upon yourself you have to see whether giving the victory to the others is going to benefit them ultimately or only temporarily. You also have to consider the effect that taking the loss upon yourself will have on your power or ability to help others in the future. It is also possible that by doing something that is harmful to others now you create a great deal of merit that will enable you to do things

---

[36] This is the sixteenth secondary vow: "The auxiliary vow to abandon not dispelling another's negative actions with wrathful methods that you know will be effective" (Lama Yeshe & Lama Zopa Rinpoche. *The Bodhisattva's Precepts: Golden Ornament of the Fortunate Ones, Pleasing All Sentient Beings.* Kopan Monastery, 1974).

vastly beneficial for others in the long run. This is another factor you have to take into account.

As Shantideva says in his *Guide*, you have to examine, both superficially and deeply, whether the benefits of doing a prohibited action outweigh the shortcomings. At times when it is difficult to tell, you should check your motivation. In his *Compendium of Buddhist Doctrine*, Shantideva says that the benefits of an action done with bodhicitta far outweigh the negativities of doing it without such motivation. Although it is extremely important, it can sometimes be very difficult to see the dividing line between what to do and what not to do, therefore you should study the texts that explain about such things. In lower texts it will say that certain actions are prohibited, while higher ones will tell you that those same actions are allowed. The more you know about all of this the easier it will be to decide what to do in any situation.[37]

6. When somebody whom I have benefited and in whom I have great hopes gives me terrible harm, I shall regard that person as my holy guru.

Usually we expect people whom we have helped a great deal to be very grateful and if they react to us with ingratitude we are likely to get angry. In such situations we should not get upset but practice patience instead. Moreover, we should see such people as teachers testing our patience and therefore treat them with respect. This verse contains all the teachings on patience found in *Guide to the Bodhisattva's Way of Life*.[38]

7. In short, both directly and indirectly, I offer every happiness and benefit to all my mothers. I shall secretly take upon myself all their harmful actions and suffering.

[37] See Shantideva, *Guide to the Bodhisattva's Way of Life*, chapter 5, and *Shiksa-Samuccaya*.
[38] Chapter 6. See also note 41, p. 161, below.

This refers to the practice of taking upon ourselves all the sufferings of others and giving away to them all our happiness, motivated by strong compassion and love. We ourselves want happiness and do not want suffering and can see that all other beings feel the same. We can see, too, that other beings are overwhelmed by suffering but do not know how to get rid of it. Thus we should generate the intention of taking on all their suffering and negative karma and pray for it to ripen upon ourselves immediately. Likewise it is obvious that other beings are devoid of the happiness they seek and do not know how to find it. Thus, without a trace of miserliness, we should offer them all our happiness—our body, wealth and merits—and pray for it to ripen on them immediately.

Of course, it is most unlikely that we shall *actually* be able to take on the sufferings of others and give them our happiness. When such transference between beings does occur, it is the result of some very strong unbroken karmic connection from the past. However, this meditation is a very powerful means of building up courage in our mind and is, therefore, a highly beneficial practice.

The *Seven Point Thought Transformation* says that we should alternate the practices of taking and giving and mount them on the breath.[39] And here, Langri Tangpa says these should be done secretly. As Shantideva's *Guide* explains, this practice does not suit the minds of beginner bodhisattvas—it is something for a select few practitioners. Therefore it is called secret.

Q. In his *Guide*, Shantideva says, "...if for the sake of others I cause harm to myself, I shall acquire all that is magnificent."[40] On the other hand, Nagarjuna says that one should not mortify the body. So, in what way does Shantideva mean one should harm oneself?

His Holiness. This does not mean that you have to hit yourself on the head or something like that. Shantideva is saying that at times

---

[39] See Geshe Rabten and Geshe Dhargyey, *Advice from a Spiritual Friend*, 92–93.
[40] Chapter 8, verse 126.

when strong, self-cherishing thoughts arise you have to argue very strongly with yourself and use forceful means to subdue them; in other words, you have to harm your self-cherishing mind. You have to distinguish clearly between the I that is completely obsessed with its own welfare and the I that is going to become enlightened: there is a big difference. And you have to see this verse of the *Guide* in the context of the verses that precede and follow it. There are many different ways the I is discussed: the grasping at a true identity for the I, the self-cherishing I, the I that we join with in looking at things from the viewpoint of others and so forth. You have to see the discussion of the self in these different contexts.

If it really benefits others, if it benefits even one sentient being, it is appropriate for us to take upon ourselves the suffering of the three realms of existence or to go to one of the hells, and we should have the courage to do this. In order to reach enlightenment for the sake of sentient beings we should be happy and willing to spend countless eons in the lowest hell, Avici. This is what is meant by taking the harms that afflict others upon ourselves.

Q. What would we have to do to get to the lowest hell?

His Holiness. The point is to develop the courage to be willing to go to one of the hells; it doesn't mean you actually have to go there. When the Kadampa geshe Chekawa was dying, he suddenly called in his disciples and asked them to make special offerings, ceremonies and prayers for him because his practice had been unsuccessful. The disciples were very upset because they thought something terrible was about to happen. However, the geshe explained that although all his life he had been praying to be born in the hells for the benefit of others, he was now receiving a pure vision of what was to follow—he was going to be reborn in a pure land instead of the hells—and that's why he was upset. In the same way, if we develop a strong, sincere wish to be reborn in the lower realms for the benefit of others, we accumulate a vast amount of merit that brings about the opposite result.

That's why I always say, if we are going to be selfish we should be wisely selfish. Real, or narrow, selfishness causes us to go down; wise selfishness brings us buddhahood. That's really wise! Unfortunately, what we usually do first is get attached to buddhahood. From the scriptures we understand that to attain buddhahood we need bodhicitta and that without it we can't become enlightened. Thus we think, "I want buddhahood, therefore I have to practice bodhicitta." We are not so much concerned about bodhicitta as about buddhahood. This is absolutely wrong. We should do the opposite; forget the selfish motivation and think how really to help others.

If we go to hell we can help neither others nor ourselves. How can we help? Not just by giving them something or performing miracles, but by teaching Dharma. However, first we must be qualified to teach. At present we cannot explain the whole path—all the practices and experiences that one person has to go through from the first stage up to the last, enlightenment. Perhaps we can explain some of the early stages through our own experience, but not much more than that. To be able to help others in the most extensive way by leading them along the entire path to enlightenment we must first enlighten ourselves. For this reason we should practice bodhicitta. This is entirely different from our usual way of thinking, where we are compelled to think of others and dedicate our heart to them because of selfish concern for our own enlightenment. This way of going about things is completely false, a sort of lie.

Q. I read in a book that just by practicing Dharma we prevent nine generations of our relatives from rebirth in hell. Is this true?

His Holiness. This is a little bit of advertising! In fact it is possible that something like this could happen, but in general it's not so simple. Take, for example, our reciting the mantra OM MANI PADME HUM and dedicating the merit of that to our rapidly attaining enlightenment for the benefit of all sentient beings. We can't say that just by reciting mantras we shall quickly attain enlightenment, but we can say that such practices act as contributory causes for enlightenment. Likewise, while our practicing Dharma will not itself protect our relatives from lower rebirths, it may act as a contributory cause for this.

If this were not the case, if our practice could act as the principal cause of a result experienced by others, it would contradict the law of karma, the relationship between cause and effect. Then we could simply sit back and relax and let all the buddhas and bodhisattvas do everything for us; we would not have to take any responsibility for our own welfare. However, the Fully Enlightened One said that all he can do is teach us the Dharma, the path to liberation from suffering, and then it's up to us to put it into practice—he washed his hands of that responsibility! As Buddhism teaches that there is no creator and that we create everything for ourselves, we are therefore our own masters—within the limits of the law of cause and effect. And this law of karma teaches that if we do good things we shall experience good results and if we do bad things we shall experience unhappiness.

Q. How do we cultivate patience?

His Holiness. There are many methods.[41] Knowledge of and faith in the law of karma themselves engender patience. You realize, "This suffering I'm experiencing is entirely my own fault, the result of actions I myself created in the past. Since I can't escape it I have to put up with it. However, if I want to avoid suffering in the future, I can do so by cultivating virtues such as patience. Getting irritated or angry with this suffering will only create negative karma, the cause for future misfortune." This is one way of practicing patience.

Another thing you can do is meditate on the suffering nature of the body: "This body and mind are the basis for all kinds of suffering; it is natural and by no means unexpected that suffering should

[41] See the Dalai Lama, *Healing Anger*, a commentary on the sixth chapter of Shantideva's *Guide.*

arise from them." This sort of realization is very helpful for the development of patience.

You can also recall what it says in Shantideva's *Guide*:

> Why be unhappy about something
> If it can be remedied?
> And what is the use of being unhappy about something
> If it cannot be remedied?[42]

If there is a method of overcoming your suffering or an opportunity to do so, you have no need to worry. If there is absolutely nothing you can do about it, worrying cannot help you at all. This is both very simple and very clear.

Something else you can do is to contemplate the disadvantages of getting angry and the advantages of practicing patience. We are human beings—one of our better qualities is our ability to think and judge. If we lose patience and get angry, we lose our ability to make proper judgments and thereby lose one of the most powerful instruments we have for tackling problems: our human wisdom. This is something that animals do not have. If we lose patience and get irritated we are damaging this precious instrument. We should remember this; it is far better to have courage and determination and face suffering with patience.

Q. How can we be humble yet at the same time realistic about the good qualities that we possess?

His Holiness. You have to differentiate between confidence in your abilities and pride. You should have confidence in whatever good qualities and skills you have and use them courageously, but you shouldn't feel arrogantly proud of them. Being humble doesn't mean feeling totally incompetent and helpless. Humility is culti-

---

[42] Chapter 6, verse 10.

vated as the opponent of pride, but we should use whatever good qualities we have to the full.

Ideally, you should have a great deal of courage and strength but not boast about or make a big show of it. Then, in times of need, you should rise to the occasion and fight bravely for what is right. This is perfect. If you have none of these good qualities but go around boasting how great you are and in times of need completely shrink back, you're just the opposite. The first person is very courageous but has no pride; the other is very proud but has no courage.

8. Undefiled by the stains of the superstitions of the eight worldly concerns, may I, by perceiving all phenomena as illusory, be released from the bondage of attachment.

This verse deals with wisdom. All the preceding practices should not be defiled by the stains of the superstitions of the eight worldly dharmas. These eight can be referred to as white, black or mixed.[43] I think it should be all right if I explain this verse from the point of view of the practices being done without their being stained by the wrong conception of clinging to true existence—the superstition of the eight worldly dharmas.[44]

---

[43] The eight worldly dharmas are attachment to (1) everything going well, (2) fame, (3) receiving material goods and (4) praise and aversion to their opposites. According to Pabongka Dechen Nyingpo, such actions are black when done with attachment to the happiness of this life, mixed when done without attachment but with self-cherishing and white when done without self-cherishing but with clinging to the I as truly existent. Another explanation has it that black are actions that both look nonvirtuous and are done with nonvirtuous motivation, mixed are actions that look virtuous but are done with nonvirtuous motivation, and white are those such as this example: a monk who is not a particularly good one acts very properly when he is in public, as if he is always like that, so that people will not criticize the Sangha. (*Footnotes 43 through 48 are from clarifications made by Lama Zopa Rinpoche.*)

[44] His Holiness chooses to explain "without their being stained" here from the point of view of the practices being done free from the wrong conception of holding things as truly existent as well as free from attachment to this life. The other way in which they can be stained is by self-cherishing.

How do we avoid staining our practice in this way? By recognizing all existence as illusory and not clinging to true existence. In this way we are liberated from the bondage of this type of clinging.

To explain the meaning of "illusory" here, true existence appears in the aspect of various objects, wherever they are manifest, but in fact there is no true existence there. True existence appears, but there is none—it is an illusion. Even though everything that exists appears as truly existent, it is devoid of true existence. To see that objects are empty of true existence—that even though true existence appears there is none, it is illusory—we should have definite understanding of the meaning of emptiness: the emptiness of the manifest appearance.

First we should be certain that all phenomena are empty of true existence. Then later, when that which has ultimate nature[45] appears to be truly existent, we refute the true existence by recalling one's previous ascertainment of the total absence of true existence. When we put together these two—the appearance of true existence and its emptiness as previously experienced—we discover the illusoriness of phenomena.

At this time there is no need for an explanation of the way things appear as illusory separate from that just given. This text explains up to the meditation on mere emptiness. In tantric teachings such as the Guhyasamaja tantra, that which is called illusory is completely separate; in this verse, that which is called illusory does not have to be shown separately. Thus, the true existence of that which has ultimate nature is the object of refutation and should be refuted. When it has been, the illusory mode of appearance of things arises indirectly: they seem to be truly existent but they are not.[46]

---

[45] "That which has ultimate nature" is the interpretive translation of the term *chos-can* used by His Holiness, where *chos* means ultimate nature.

[46] A mirage appears to be water but it is not. When we understand the reality that what we are seeing is an optical illusion caused by atmospheric conditions, we still see the water but it appears illusory.

Q. How can something that is unfindable and exists merely by imputation function?

His Holiness. That's very difficult. If you can realize that subject and action exist by reason of their being dependent arisings, emptiness will appear in dependent arising. This is the most difficult thing to understand.[47]

If you have realized non-inherent existence well, the experience of existent objects speaks for itself. That they exist by nature is refuted by logic, and you can be convinced by logic that things do not—there is no way that they can—inherently exist. Yet they definitely do exist because we experience them. So how do they exist? They exist merely by the power of name. This is not saying that they don't exist; it is never said that things do not exist. What is said is that they exist by the power of name. This is a difficult point; something that you can understand slowly, slowly through experience.

First you have to analyze whether things exist truly or not, actually findably or not: you can't find them. But if we say that they don't exist at all, this is a mistake, because we do experience them. We can't prove through logic that things exist findably, but we do know through our experience that they exist. Thus we can make a definite conclusion that things do exist. Now, if things exist there are only two ways in which they can do so: either from their own base or by being under the control of other factors, that is, either completely

---

[47] Take, for example, "I am going to Kathmandu." How are the subject I, and the action, going, dependent arisings? Why do you say, "I am going"? Your aggregates are going to Kathmandu and you merely label them I—the subject is dependent upon the aggregates, as are the subject's actions. When you consider how the I exists dependent upon being imputed by thought to its basis, the aggregates, and how actions too depend upon thought and the basis of imputation, you can see the subject and the action as dependent arisings. While you reflect on this—that subject and action exist dependent upon the aggregates (the basis of imputation), the label and the thought—you lose the truly existent I on the aggregates and the truly existent I going to Kathmandu. By realizing that the aggregates are empty of the truly existent I and its action of going, you automatically realize that the I and its actions exist dependent upon the aggregates and their actions, and by the power of name.

independently or dependently. Since logic disproves that things exist independently, the only way they can exist is dependently.

Upon what do things depend for their existence? They depend upon the base that is labeled and the thought that labels. If they could be found when searched for, they should exist by their own nature, and thus the Madhyamaka scriptures, which say that things do not exist by their own nature, would be wrong. However, things cannot be found when searched for. What is found is something that exists under the control of other factors, which is therefore said to exist merely in name. The word "merely" here indicates that something is being cut off: but what is being cut off is not the name, nor is it that which has a meaning and is the object of a valid mind. We are not saying that there is no meaning to things other than their names, or that the meaning that is not the name is not the object of a valid mind. What it cuts off is that it exists by something other than the power of name. Things exist merely by the power of name, but they have meaning, and that meaning is the object of a valid mind. But the nature of things is that they exist simply by the power of name.

There is no other alternative, only the force of name. That does not mean that besides the name there is nothing. There is the thing, there is a meaning and there is a name. What is the meaning? The meaning also exists merely in name.

Q. Is the mind something that really exists or is it also an illusion?

His Holiness. It's the same thing. According to the Prasangika Madhyamaka, the highest, most precise view, it's the same thing whether it is an external object or the internal consciousness that apprehends it: both exist by the power of name; neither is truly existent. Thought itself exists merely in name; so do emptiness, buddha, good, bad and indifferent. Everything exists solely by the power of name.

When we say "name only" there is no way to understand what it means other than that it cuts off meanings that are not name only. If you take a real person and a phantom person, for example, both are the same in that they exist merely by name, but there is a difference between them. Whatever exists or does not exist is merely labeled, but in name, some things exist and others do not.[48]

According to the Mind Only school, external phenomena appear to inherently exist but are, in fact, empty of external, inherent existence, whereas the mind is truly existent. I think this is enough about Buddhist tenets for now.[49]

Q. Are "mind" and "consciousness" equivalent terms?

His Holiness. There are distinctions made in Tibetan, but it's difficult to say whether the English words carry the same connotations. Where "mind" refers to primary consciousness it would probably be the same as "consciousness." In Tibetan, "awareness" is the most general term and is divided into primary consciousness and (secondary) mental factors, both of which have many further subdivisions. Also, when we speak of awareness there are mental and sensory awareness, and the former has many subdivisions into various degrees of roughness and subtlety. Whether or not the English words correspond to the Tibetan in terms of precision and so forth is difficult to say.

---

[48] The real person and the phantom person are both merely labeled, but the real person actually exists because his basis of imputation, the aggregates that are labeled "person," exists. The phantom person does not exist because there are no aggregates, no consciousness for him to depend on; he does not exist in name. In a dream, the appearance of a person serves as a basis of imputation but it is not a proper base as there are no aggregates.

[49] For more on tenets, see Geshe Sopa and Jeffrey Hopkins, *Cutting Through Appearances*, and Daniel Cozort and Craig Preston, *Buddhist Philosophy*.

DEVELOPING SINGLE-POINTED CONCENTRATION

Gelek Rimpoche

L AMA TSONGKHAPA taught that we should practice both contemplative meditation and concentration meditation. In the former we investigate the object of meditation by contemplating it in all its details; in the latter we focus single-pointedly on one aspect of the object and hold our mind on it without movement.

Single-pointed concentration—*samadhi* in Sanskrit—is a meditative power that is useful in either of these two types of meditation. However, in order to develop samadhi itself we must cultivate principally concentration meditation. In terms of practice, this means that we must choose an object of concentration and then meditate single-pointedly on it every day until the power of samadhi is attained.

The five great obstacles to samadhi are (1) laziness, (2) forgetfulness, (3) mental wandering and mental sinking, (4) failure to correct any of the above problems when they arise and, finally, (5) applying meditative opponents to problems that are not there; that is, they are purely imaginary.

LAZINESS

The actual antidote to laziness is an initial experience of the pleasure and harmony of body and mind that arise from meditation. Once we experience this joy, meditation automatically becomes one of our favorite activities. However, until we get to this point we must settle for a lesser antidote to laziness—something that will counteract our laziness and encourage us to practice until the experience of meditative ecstasy comes to us. This lesser antidote is contemplation of the benefits of samadhi.

What are these benefits? Among them are attaining siddhis very quickly, transforming sleep into profound meditation and being able to read others' minds, see into the future, remember past incarnations and perform magical acts such as flying and levitating. Contemplating these benefits helps eliminate laziness.

FORGETFULNESS

The second obstacle to samadhi is forgetfulness—simply losing awareness of the object of meditation. When this happens, concentration is no longer present. Nagarjuna illustrated the process of developing concentration by likening the mind to an elephant to be tied by the rope of memory to the pillar of the object of meditation. The meditator also carries the iron hook of wisdom with which to spur on the lazy elephant.

What should we choose as an object of meditation? It can be anything—a stone, fire, a piece of wood, a table and so forth—as long as it does not cause delusions such as desire or aversion to arise. We should also avoid an object that has no qualities specifically significant to our spiritual path. Some teachers have said that we should begin with fire and later change to swirling clouds and so forth, but this is not an effective approach. Choose one object and stick to it.

Many people choose the symbolic form of a buddha or a meditational deity as their object. The former has many benefits and is a great blessing; the latter provides a special preparation for higher tantric practice. In the beginning we can place a statue or painting of the object of meditation in front of us and look at it as we concentrate. But as it is our mind, not our eyes, that we want to develop, this should be done only until familiarity with the object is gained. The most important point is to settle on one object and not change it. There are stories of great saints who chose the form of a yak as their object but generally it is better to select an object of greater spiritual value and not change it until at least the first of the four levels of samadhi is attained.

Consistency in practice is also important. Once we begin we should continue every day until we reach our goal. If the conditions are perfect, we can do this in three months or so. But practicing an hour a day for a month and then missing a day or two will result in minimal progress. Constant, steady effort is necessary. We need to follow a fixed daily schedule of meditation.

Let's say our object of concentration is the symbolic form of the Buddha. The first problem is that we cannot immediately visualize the form clearly. The advice is this: don't be concerned with details—just get a sort of yellowish blur and hold it in mind. At this stage you can use an external image as an aid, alternating between looking at the object and then trying to hold it in mind for a few moments without looking. Forgetfulness, the second of the five obstacles, is very strong at this point and we must struggle against it. Get a mental picture of the object and then hold it firmly. Whenever it fades away, forcefully bring it back.

WANDERING AND MENTAL SINKING

However, this forceful holding of the object can give rise to the third problem. When we try to hold the object in the mind, the tension of this effort can produce either agitation or mental sinking. The forced concentration produces a heaviness of mind and this in turn leads to sleep, which itself is a coarse form of mental sinking. The subtle form of mental sinking is experienced when we are able to hold the object in mind for a prolonged period of time but without any real clarity. Without clarity, the meditation lacks strength.

To illustrate this with an example: when a man in love thinks of his beloved, her face immediately appears radiantly in his mind and effortlessly remains with clarity. A few months later, however, when they are in the middle of a fight, he has to strain to think of her in the same way. When he had the tightness of desire the image was easy to retain clearly. This tightness is called close placement.[50] When close placement is lost, the image eventually disappears and subtle mental sinking sets in. It is very difficult to distinguish between proper meditation and meditation characterized by subtle mental sinking, but remaining absorbed in the latter can create many problems.

We must also guard against the second problem, mentally wan-

---

[50] Skt: *satipatthana*; Tib: *nyer-zhag*.

dering away from the object of meditation. Most people sit down to concentrate on an object but their mind quickly drifts away to thoughts of the day's activities, a movie or television program they recently saw or something like that.

Pabongka Rinpoche, the root guru of both tutors of the present Dalai Lama, used to tell the story of a very important Tibetan government official who would always put a pen and a notebook beside his meditation seat whenever he did his daily practices, saying that his best ideas came from mental wandering in meditation.

Our mind wanders off on some memory or plan and we don't even realize that it's happening. We think we are still meditating but suddenly realize that for the past thirty minutes our mind has been somewhere else. This is the coarse level of wandering mind. When we have overcome this we still have to deal with subtle wandering, in which one factor of the mind holds the object clearly but another factor drifts away. We have to develop the ability of using the main part of our mind to concentrate on the object and another part to watch that the meditation is progressing correctly. This side part of the mind is like a secret agent and without it we can become absorbed in incorrect meditation for hours without knowing what we are doing—the thief of mental wandering or mental sinking comes in and steals away our meditation.

We have to watch, but not over-watch. Over-watching can create another problem. It is like when we hold a glass of water: we have to hold it, hold it tightly, and also watch to see that we are holding it correctly and steadily without allowing any water to spill out. Holding, holding tightly and watching: these are the three keys of samadhi meditation.

FAILURE TO CORRECT PROBLEMS

The fourth problem is failure to correct problems such as mental sinking or wandering. The antidote to depression is tightening the concentration; the antidote to wandering is loosening it.

When counteracting mental sinking with tightness, we must be careful to avoid the excessive tightness that a lack of natural desire to meditate can create; we have to balance tightness with relaxation. When our mind gets too tight like this we should just relax within our meditation. If that doesn't work, we can forget the object for a while and concentrate on happy thoughts, such as the beneficial effects of bodhicitta, until our mind regains its composure, and then return to our object of meditation. This is akin to washing our face in cold water.

If contemplating a happy subject does not pick us up, we can visualize that our mind takes the form of a tiny seed at our heart and then shoot this seed out of the crown of our head into the clouds above, leave it there for a few moments and then bring it back. If this doesn't help, we can just take a short break from our meditation.

Similarly, when mental wandering arises, we can think of an unpleasant subject, such as the suffering nature of samsara.

When our mind is low, changing to a happy subject can bring it back up; when it's wandering, changing to an unpleasant subject can bring it down out of the sky and back to earth.

CORRECTING NON-EXISTENT PROBLEMS

The fifth obstacle is applying antidotes to mental sinking or wandering that are not present or overly watching for problems. This hinders the development of our meditation.

THE MEDITATION POSTURE

The posture recommended for meditation is the seven-point posture of Buddha Vairochana. Sit on a comfortable cushion in the vajra posture with both legs crossed and your soles upturned. Indians call this the lotus posture; Tibetans call it the vajra posture. It is the first of the seven features of the Vairochana posture. If you find this or any of the other points difficult, simply sit as is most convenient and comfortable.

The seven-point posture is actually the most effective position for meditation once you develop familiarity and comfort with it, but until then, if one of the points is too difficult you can substitute it with something more within your reach.

Keep your back straight and tilt your head slightly forward with your eyes cast down along the line of your nose. If your eyes are cast too high, mental wandering is facilitated; if too low, sleepiness or mental sinking too easily set in. Don't close your eyes but look down along the line of your nose to an imaginary point about five feet in front of you. In order not to be distracted by environmental objects, many meditators sit facing a blank wall. Keep your shoulders level, your teeth lightly closed and place the tip of the tongue against the front of your hard palate just behind your top teeth, which will prevent you from getting thirsty when engaging in prolonged meditation.

THE MEDITATION SESSION

Start your meditation session with a prayer to the lineage gurus in connection with your visualization. Then go directly to concentrating on your chosen object, such as an image of the Buddha.

At first, your main difficulty will be to get hold of the mental image; even getting a blurred image is difficult. However, you have to persist.

Once you have succeeded, you have to cultivate clarity and the correct level of tightness, while guarding against problems such as wandering, mental sinking and so forth. Just sit and pursue the meditation while watching for distortions. Sometimes the object becomes too clear and you break into mental wandering; at other times it becomes dull and you lose it to sleep or torpor. In this

way, using the six powers and the four connecting principles,[51] you
can overcome the five obstacles and ascend the nine stages to calm
abiding, where you can meditate effortlessly and ecstatically for as
long as you want.

In the beginning, your main struggle will be against wandering
and mental sinking. Just look for the object and as soon as you
notice a problem, correct it. On the ninth stage, even though you
can concentrate effortlessly for a great length of time, you have not
yet attained samadhi. First you must also develop a certain sense
of pleasure and harmony within both body and mind. Concentrate
until a great pleasure begins to arise within your head and spreads
down, feeling like the gentle invigorating warmth of a hot towel
held against your face. The pleasure spreads throughout your body
until you feel as light as cotton. Meditate within this physical pleasure, which gives rise to mental ecstasy. Then when you meditate
you have a sense of inseparability with the object—your body seems
to disappear in meditation and you sort of become one with the
object; you almost want to fly away in your meditation. After this
you can fix your mind on any object of virtue for as long you want.
This is the preparatory stage, or the first level of samadhi. Meditation is light and free, like a humming bird in mid-air drinking nectar
from a red flower.

Beyond this you can either remain in samadhi meditation
and cultivate the four levels of samadhi or, as advised by Lama
Tsongkhapa, turn to searching for the root of samsara. No matter
how high your samadhi, if you do not cut the root of samsara, you
will eventually fall.

Lama Tsongkhapa likened samadhi to a horse ridden by a warrior and the wisdom that cuts the root of samsara to the warrior's
sword. When you have gained the first level of samadhi you have
found the horse and can then turn to the sword of wisdom. Unless
you gain the sword of wisdom your attainment of samadhi will

[51] See the Dalai Lama, *Opening the Eye of New Awareness*, 53–66.

be prone to collapse. You can take rebirth in one of the seventeen realms of the gods of form but eventually you will fall. On the other hand, if you develop basic samadhi and then apply it to the development of wisdom you'll be able to cut the root of samsara as quickly as a crow takes out the eyes of an enemy. Once you've cut this root, you are beyond falling.

Gelek Rimpoche (1939–) was born in Tibet and studied at Drepung Monastery and later in India, where he gained his lharampa geshe degree. In the 1980s, after publishing many important texts and teaching Dharma in India, he came to the USA, where, based in Ann Arbor, Michigan, he is now spiritual head of the Jewel Heart Buddhist centers in America and abroad. This teaching was given at Tushita Mahayana Meditation Centre, 25 April 1980, and first published in *Teachings at Tushita* in 1981.

In Search of the Self

Geshe Ngawang Dhargyey

W E ALL SUFFER; many sentient beings experience almost constant misery. However, at present we have the time, space and ability to think about how to get rid of all suffering—not get over just one problem or become a little more peaceful, but completely finish with suffering altogether.

We humans have many methods of finding happiness at our disposal but even though we live in beautiful houses crammed full of all kinds of stuff we are still not satisfied. That's because there is only one thing that can really eradicate dissatisfaction and bring true happiness: the practice of Dharma.

If we check within ourselves we will discover that all our misery comes from either attachment or hatred. These, in turn, come from an incorrect view of the self. Even at this moment we hold the I to be true. In his *Guide to the Middle Way*, Chandrakirti stated that all emotional afflictions arise from ignorance—misapprehension of the nature of the self. This is the root. In order to get rid of all the branches of suffering and prevent them from ever arising again, we need to sever this root. In this way we can put an end to all misery, even birth, sickness, aging and death.

The Buddha's main teachings on eradicating ignorance by understanding and realizing the wisdom of non-self-existence are found in his *Perfection of Wisdom (Prajnaparamita) Sutras*, and these texts are the main scriptural source for the great sage Nagarjuna's *Six-fold Canon of Reasoning*, especially his *Fundamental Verses on the Middle Way (Mulamadhyamakakarika)*. Other teachings on the wisdom realizing emptiness may be found in Aryadeva's *Four Hundred Verses (Catuhsaka)*; Buddhapalita's famous *Commentary on [Nagarjuna's] Treatise on the Middle Way (Buddhapalita-Mulamamadhyamakavrtti)*; Chandrakirti's *Clear Phrases (Prasannapada)*; and the ninth chapter of Shantideva's *Guide to the Bodhisattva's Way of Life*.

The essence of all the techniques found in these and other scriptures for developing an understanding of the emptiness of self-existence is the method called the "Four Essential Points," or the "Four Keys." These provide a very effective approach to emptiness. We begin by applying these four methods of analysis to gain an understanding of the selflessness of persons and then use them to gain an understanding of the selflessness of phenomena.

THE FIRST ESSENTIAL POINT

The first of the four keys is called "the essential point of ascertaining the object to be eliminated." We cannot realize emptiness without first knowing what it is that things are empty of; emptiness is not just a vague nothingness. This first point helps us understand how the false self—the object to be refuted and eliminated—exists. We need to recognize how we view the I as inherently existent, as if it were independent of the aggregates of body and mind. The I appears to be substantially established, existent in its own right, and this mode of existence does not appear to be imposed by our own mental projection.

The way we hold and believe the I to exist becomes particularly clear when we're angry or afraid. At such times we should analyze how the self appears to our mind; how our mind apprehends it. We can provoke these emotions in meditation and, while maintaining them, use a subtle part of our consciousness to recognize how we conceive our I.

In order to catch a thief we have to know who the person is and what he or she looks like. The greatest thief of all is our mistaken sense of self—the conception that not only ourselves but all other phenomena as well are truly existent. We believe that things really exist the way they appear to our senses, as objectively established, as existing from their own side. This, then, is what we have to know in order to catch this great thief, who steals all our happiness and peace of mind.

If we do not recognize this wrong conception and simply walk around saying, "Emptiness! Emptiness!" we are likely to fall into one of the two extremes of eternalism or nihilism—believing either that things are inherently existent or that nothing exists at all, thus exaggerating or denying conventional reality.

Therefore, we must recognize the false self, the object of refutation, before we can start actually refuting, or eliminating, it. This is the initial step in developing an understanding of emptiness and the foundation of realizing it. First we must look for the false self, not selflessness. This requires a great deal of meditation.

For our meditation on emptiness to be effective, we need to prepare our mind by purifying negativities and accumulating merit. The essence of purification and creation of merit is the practice of the seven limbs of prostration, offering, confessing, rejoicing, beseeching, requesting and dedicating. We can also engage in preliminaries such as making 100,000 mandala offerings, Vajrasattva mantra recitations and so forth.

When we start observing how the false self—the self we have habitually assumed to exist in persons and objects—manifests, we soon discover that it does not exist at all. Before we begin cultivating this awareness, our I seems to really be there, very solidly, but as soon as we start checking, we cannot find it. It disappears. If the I truly did exist, the more we searched for it the more concrete it should become...we should at least be able to find it. If it can't be found, how can it exist?

THE SECOND ESSENTIAL POINT

The inherently existent I must exist as either one with the body and mind—that is, identical with them—or separate from them. There is no third way in which it can exist. This is the second of the four keys, ascertaining the logical pervasion of the two possibilities of sameness or difference.

We have to watch for the self-existent I, which appears to be established independently, as if it were not created by the mind.

If the self does not exist as it appears, we should not believe in it. Perhaps we think it's someplace else—that it will show up when we meet our guru or that it's floating around outside the window somewhere. But we need to understand that there's no third alternative. Therefore, we have to meditate on the second key with awareness that if this apparent I is neither identical with nor separate from the five aggregates of body and mind, there's no way it can exist. At this point it becomes easy for us to understand the general character of emptiness.

THE THIRD ESSENTIAL POINT

The third key is ascertaining the absence of true sameness of the I and the five aggregates. Once we have ascertained the object of refutation by meditating on emptiness and seen how it cannot exist in a way other than as one with the five aggregates or separate from them, we concentrate on whether or not the self-existent I *can* exist as one with the five aggregates.

If the I is the same as the aggregates, then because there are five aggregates, there must be five continuums of the I or, because the I is one, the five aggregates must be an indivisible whole. We therefore examine each aggregate to see if it is the same as the self. We ask, "Are my self and my body the same?" "Are my self and my feelings the same?" "Are my self and my discriminating awareness the same?" And so forth.

There are many different analytical procedures to show that the concept of the self as one with the psychophysical aggregates is wrong. I can deal with them only briefly here. For example, if the self were a permanent entity, as self-existence implies, destroying it would be impossible. Then, if the I were the same as the body, the body could never die and the corpse could never be burned, because this would destroy the self. This is obviously nonsensical.

Also, the mind and body would be unchanging, because that is the nature of a substantial self. Furthermore, if there were a self-existent I identical with the body and the mind, it would be one indistinguishable entity and the individual designations of "my body" and "my mind" would be incorrect.

Thus, there are many different ways we can reason and meditate upon to arrive at the conclusion that reality and our habitual way of perceiving things are completely different. We are not fixed, permanent entities.

THE FOURTH ESSENTIAL POINT

Having ascertained, as above, that the self and the aggregates are not a true unity, we then consider whether or not our self-existent I is different from and unrelated to the aggregates. This is the fourth key, ascertaining the absence of any true difference between the self and the aggregates.

For example, if you have a sheep, a goat and an ox, you can find the ox by taking away the sheep and the goat. Similarly, if the I existed separately from the body and the mind, when we eliminated the body and the mind we would be left with a third entity to represent the "I." But when we search outside of our body, feelings, consciousness and so forth we come up with nothing. Generations of yogis have found that there is nothing to be found beyond the aggregates.

Once more, there are many different ways to reason when contemplating the possibility that the self is separate from the aggregates. If they were truly different, there would be no connection between them. If we said, for example, "My head aches," the "my" would refer to something other than the "head" (the form aggregate) and "ache" (the feeling aggregate); it would be something that existed somewhere else. The aggregate would hurt, not me. If the self were truly a different thing, a true polarity apart from the aggregates, it would be absurd to say, "My head hurts," "My hand hurts" and so forth, as though the pain somehow affected the self.

By performing different kinds of analysis we cultivate the certainty that the self and the aggregates are not truly different.

MEDITATION ON EMPTINESS

Since these four keys contain the essential points of Nagarjuna's main treatises on the Middle Way, they make it easy to meditate on emptiness.

If we meditate with the four keys to search for the self in our body, from the top of our head to the tips of our toes, and our aggregates of mind as well, we won't find anything. Thus, we will come to the realization that a fixed, unchanging self does not exist. It's like looking for a cow in a certain field. We walk all around: up the hills, down the valleys, through the trees, everywhere. Having searched the entire area and found nothing, we arrive at the certainty that the cow simply isn't there. Similarly, when we investigate the aggregates of body and mind and find nothing, we arrive at the certainty that the self-existent I simply isn't there either. This is the understanding of emptiness.

We then concentrate single-pointedly on the experience of the absence of the self that we had always presumed to exist. Whenever this certainty begins to weaken or lose clarity, we return to our analytical meditation and again check through the four keys. Once more a sharpness of certainty arises and we return to concentrating on it single-pointedly. In this way we cultivate two things: the certainty of finding nothing there and the subjective experience of how this appears. By keeping these two together and not allowing our mind to wander we reach what is called the single-pointed concentration of balanced space-like absorption, wherein everything appears non-dual. Subject and object merge like water poured into water.

We also have to learn what to do when we arise from meditation—in the post-meditation period we have to view everything that appears as illusory. Even though things appear to be self-existent, they are simply the sport of emptiness, like a magician's creations. This state is called the samadhi of illusory manifestations.

Our practice should alternate in this way between the samadhi of space-like absorption and that of illusory manifestation, thus avoiding the extremes of absolutism and nihilism. This activates the mental factor called ecstasy and we experience intense physical and mental ease. Our meditation just seems to take off on its own without requiring any effort. Once this ecstasy is activated, the power of our meditation increases one hundred times and we achieve penetrative insight into emptiness.

We should spend a great deal of time meditating on the four keys. It may be difficult but it is the most powerful and beneficial form of meditation for counteracting delusions. As Aryadeva said, "Even doubting the validity of inherent existence rips samsara to shreds."[52]

Meditation on emptiness is the most powerful way to purify negative karma. During Guru Shakyamuni Buddha's time there was a king who had killed his own father. He was terrified that this evil act would cause him to be reborn in hell and asked the Buddha for advice. The Buddha instructed him to meditate on emptiness. The king devoted himself to this practice and was able to purify that negative karma from his mindstream.

After Lama Tsongkhapa attained enlightenment he wrote the poem *In Praise of the Buddha's Teaching on Dependent Arising*, in which he stated that although all of the Buddha's teachings are beneficial and undeceiving, the most beneficial and undeceiving, the most miraculously wonderful, is his teaching on emptiness, because by meditating on it sentient beings can cut the root of samsara and attain liberation from all suffering. In awe and amazement, Lama

---

[52] Aryadeva's *Four Hundred*, verse 180:

Those with little merit
Do not even doubt this teaching [on emptiness].
Entertaining just a doubt
Tears to tatters worldly existence.
See Aryadeva and Gyel-tsap, *Yogic Deeds of Bodhisattvas*, 188.

Tsongkhapa thus praised the Buddha's uncanny perceptiveness and reliability of knowledge as both a scientist and philosopher.

When we understand that the Buddha really did know and describe the true nature of reality by means of his teachings on emptiness, firm faith arises within us. This faith is not based upon stories or fantasy but upon the experience that arises by practicing and realizing the situation for ourselves. We find that reality exists exactly the way the Buddha described it. Furthermore, he discovered this reality a long, long time ago, without the need of so-called scientific instruments.

Geshe Ngawang Dhargyey (1921–95) was born in the Trehor district of Kham in eastern Tibet and studied at the local Dhargye Monastery until he was eighteen, when he went to Sera Monastery, in Lhasa. He went into exile in 1959 and in 1971 was appointed chief Dharma teacher at the Library of Tibetan Works and Archives. He remained there until he moved to New Zealand in 1985, where he passed away ten years later. He gave this teaching at Tushita Mahayana Meditation Centre, 2 January 1980. It was edited from an oral translation by Robert Thurman and first published in *Teachings at Tushita* in 1981.

The Foundation of All Good Qualities [53]

Khunu Lama Rinpoche

UNKNOWN

[53] Tib: *Yön-ten-shir-gyur-ma*. See appendix 4 for a translation of the root text.

THE ULTIMATE PURPOSE of listening to teachings is to receive enlightenment. Therefore, before listening to this teaching on the *Foundation of All Good Qualities* it is necessary to cultivate the pure thought of bodhicitta, the main cause of enlightenment.

We receive enlightenment only by practicing Dharma. Without practicing Dharma there's no way to receive enlightenment. Enlightenment can be received only through the practice of Dharma.

There are two types of Dharma, outer and inner. Inner Dharma means Buddhadharma; outer Dharma refers to the non-Buddhist religions, the religions followed by non-Buddhists. Of these, there are five divisions.[54] By practicing outer Dharma, you can receive only temporary, samsaric pleasures but you cannot receive enlightenment. To become enlightened, you have to practice inner Dharma, Buddhadharma.

With respect to Buddhadharma, there are four schools of philosophical thought: Vaibhashika, Sautrantika, Cittamatra and Madhyamaka. These four schools encompass the two main divisions of Buddhadharma, the Hinayana and the Mahayana. Vaibhashika and Sautrantika are Hinayana schools; Cittamatra and Madhyamaka are Mahayana. The teachings that we should practice are those of the Mahayana; in particular, those of the Middle Way, the Madhyamaka school, whose view is the best, most perfect and pure. But while the view of the Madhyamaka school is purer than that of the Cittamatra and is that which we should study, when it comes to extensive action, or skillful means, the teachings of the Cittamatra and the Madhyamaka are the same. The Madhyamaka, therefore, contains the best teachings on both profound view and extensive conduct.

Lama Tsongkhapa's *Great Treatise on the Stages of the Path* elaborates in great detail the steps of the sutra, or Paramitayana, path,

[54] See Hopkins, *Meditation on Emptiness*, 317–33.

but when it comes to the Vajrayana, it states simply that we should enter this path; it doesn't explain the graded path of tantra in detail, as it does the sutra path.[55]

The short text by Lama Tsongkhapa that we're going to talk about here, the *Foundation of All Good Qualities*, is rooted in the Madhyamaka teachings and it is therefore very important that you understand it.

The first verse reads,

> The foundation of all good qualities is the kind and perfect,
>   pure guru;
> Correct devotion to him is the root of the path.
> By clearly seeing this and applying great effort,
> Please bless me to rely upon him with great respect.

This verse, obviously, is about guru practice. All the good qualities of liberation, the boundless state, and enlightenment, the ultimate goal, depend upon the guru. Therefore it is necessary to find a perfect guru who has all the qualities explained in the lam-rim teachings.[56] Our responsibility as disciples is to follow the guru's instructions exactly, offer service, make prostrations and so forth. By following the perfect guru perfectly, we can receive enlightenment. If, instead, we follow a misleading guide, a false teacher, all we'll receive is rebirth in one of the lower realms such as the hells.

Why do we need a guru? Because we're trying to reach enlightenment and don't know what it is. The guru knows what enlightenment is. Therefore, we need to find and then follow a guru. Since the extremely kind and venerable guru is the foundation of all good qualities—the good qualities of liberation and enlightenment—the

---

[55] Lama Tsongkhapa details the tantric path in his *Great Treatise on the Stages of Mantra*.

[56] See Lama Zopa Rinpoche, *Heart of the Path*, for extensive teachings on guru devotion.

first thing we must do is to find a perfectly qualified guru. Then we must follow that guru correctly by making material offerings, offering respect and service and doing whatever else should be done. But the main thing, the most important thing, the essence of following the guru correctly, is to follow the guru's instructions exactly.

Although short, this text, *The Foundation of All Good Qualities*, explains the entire graduated path, including the six perfections, especially the perfection of wisdom, and the necessity of entering the Vajrayana path. The next verse, then, explains the difficulty of receiving a perfect human rebirth. It reads,

> Understanding that the precious freedom of this rebirth is
>   found only once,
> Is greatly meaningful and difficult to find again,
> Please bless me to generate the mind that unceasingly,
> Day and night, takes its essence.

Since beginningless time, in numberless bodies, we have been wandering through the six samsaric realms, but this is the one time that we have received a perfect human rebirth. A rebirth such as this, which is free from the eight unfree states and possessed of the ten richnesses, will be extremely difficult to find again. We can see how rare it is by meditating in three ways: on cause, example and number. It's hard enough to find an ordinary human rebirth let alone one with these eight freedoms and ten richnesses; the perfect human rebirth is much harder to find than a regular one.

This perfect human rebirth gives us the chance of continuing to be reborn in the realms of suffering or of attaining enlightenment; it offers every possibility. Therefore, it is highly significant. What we should use it for is attaining enlightenment—since we have received a perfect human rebirth just this once, we should use it to attain enlightenment. Therefore, the teaching says, "Please bless me to generate the mind that unceasingly, day and night, takes its essence."

The next verse tells us that the perfect human rebirth is not only difficult to find but also decays very quickly, like a water bubble:

> This life is as impermanent as a water bubble;
> Remember how quickly it decays and death comes.
> After death, just like a shadow follows the body,
> The results of black and white karma follow.

Death is certain but when it will arrive is not. One thing that's for sure is that we are not going to live for one hundred years. One hundred years from now, pretty much everybody alive today will be dead. It is very important to remember impermanence. The Kadampa geshes used to remember impermanence all the time in order to avoid seeking the comfort of the temporal life. They felt that if they didn't bring it to mind in the morning they were in danger of wasting the entire afternoon, and if they didn't bring it to mind in the afternoon they were in danger of wasting the whole night. By constantly keeping impermanence in mind, they were able to prevent the meaningless thought seeking only the comfort of this life from arising.

After death, our mind doesn't come to a complete stop, like water drying up or a flame going out. There is continuity. Just as wherever the body goes the shadow comes along with it, similarly, wherever our mind goes our karma comes along too. You must have unshakably firm belief in this.

With respect to karma, there are the ten nonvirtuous actions and the ten virtuous ones. We must avoid the former and practice the latter. Thus the teaching says,

> Finding firm and definite conviction in this,
> Please bless me always to be careful
> To abandon even the slightest negativities
> And accomplish all virtuous deeds.

In other words, "Please bless me always to be careful in the practice of avoiding the ten nonvirtuous actions and observing the ten virtuous ones."

The next verse tells us that no matter how much we enjoy samsaric pleasures, there's no way to find satisfaction in them.

> Seeking samsaric pleasures is the door to all suffering:
> They are uncertain and cannot be relied upon.
> Recognizing these shortcomings,
> Please bless me to generate the strong wish for the bliss of
>   liberation.

Whatever beautiful objects we see, we're never satisfied; whatever pleasant sounds we hear, we're never satisfied; and it's the same with all other objects of the senses. No matter how many television programs or movies we see, we'll never be satisfied. This is how it is, and all samsaric pleasures are the door to samsaric suffering. No matter how many samsaric pleasures there are, they are of no value. All past great meditators and holy beings have recognized temporal pleasure as a shortcoming of samsara; as faulty, deceptive. They have never seen samsaric pleasure as valuable or good.

> Led by this pure thought,
> Mindfulness, alertness and great caution arise.
> The root of the teachings is keeping the pratimoksha vows:
> Please bless me to accomplish this essential practice.

With this next verse, we request blessings to succeed in the essential practice of keeping the vows of individual liberation. There are seven different levels of pratimoksha ordination, such as fully ordained monk or nun,[57] and keeping the pratimoksha vows is root of the teaching and the main cause of liberation. Supported by the

---

[57] Skt: *bhikshu*; Tib: *gelong*, and Skt: *bhikshuni*; Tib: *gelongma* respectively.

pure thought of wanting to receive nirvana, we should keep our precepts with great remembrance, conscientiousness and care.

We shouldn't be like those practitioners who say that they're focusing on tantric practice and therefore don't need to concern themselves with sutra practices, like keeping the pratimoksha vows. We should observe whatever pratimoksha vows we have taken with great care. First it is necessary to generate the mind wanting to abandon samsara. Without renunciation of samsara, we cannot receive even Hinayana nirvana—the liberation of the *Shravakayana* and *Pratyekabuddhayana*.

Then, after generating the mind renouncing samsara, it is necessary to generate bodhicitta. Without bodhicitta we cannot receive enlightenment. Therefore, it is necessary to practice bodhicitta. The next verse reads,

> Just as I have fallen into the sea of samsara,
> So have all mother migratory beings.
> Please bless me to see this, train in supreme bodhicitta,
> And bear the responsibility of freeing migratory beings.

Look at yourself. Since beginningless time, you have been suffering incredibly by wandering endlessly through the various realms of cyclic existence—mainly the hell, preta and animal realms—and just as you have been suffering in samsara since beginningless time, so too have all other samsaric sentient beings. Thinking in this way, cultivate bodhicitta, or, as the prayer says, "Please bless me to receive bodhicitta by understanding this."

> Even if I develop only bodhicitta, but I don't practice
>   the three types of morality,
> I will not achieve enlightenment.
> With my clear recognition of this,
> Please bless me to practice the bodhisattva vows with
>   great energy.

In order to receive aspirational bodhicitta, the thought wishing to receive enlightenment for the sake of all sentient beings, and engaging bodhicitta, actually following the path to enlightenment, it is necessary to practice the three aspects of the perfection of morality—the morality of abstaining from negativity, the morality of creating all virtue and the morality of working for sentient beings. Although this verse mentions specifically the three divisions of morality, it also refers to the practice of all six perfections.

However, the following verse refers more specifically to the last two perfections, concentration and wisdom.

> Once I have pacified distractions to wrong objects
> And correctly analyzing the meaning of reality,
> Please bless me to generate quickly within my mindstream
> The unified path of calm abiding and special insight.

Here Lama Tsongkhapa is saying that our mind is always distracted by objects of the senses, for example, attractive visual forms or interesting sounds. Our mind is always concentrated on those. Calm abiding, or mental quiescence (*shamatha*), is a kind of reversal of our normal attraction to sense objects, the opposite of distraction—it is the control of single-pointed concentration. *Shama* means peace; *tha* means one-pointedness. This is to be combined with penetrative insight. In Tibetan, the phrase *yang-dag-par-jog-pa* means concentrating on ultimate nature. In this prayer, Lama Tsongkhapa asks for blessings to quickly achieve the path that unifies shamatha and *vipashyana*. When we achieve this path, we are close to enlightenment.

Up to this point, Lama Tsongkhapa has been talking about the general training of the mind in the Paramitayana path. Next, he talks about tantra:

> Having become a pure vessel by training in the general path,
> Please bless me to enter

The holy gateway of the fortunate ones:
The supreme vajra vehicle.

In other words, he's saying here, "Please bless me to achieve the Vajrayana path, which allows me to receive enlightenment in this lifetime." If you follow the general, Paramitayana, path it can take you a long time to collect the necessary merit and reach enlightenment, as long as three countless great eons. Guru Shakyamuni Buddha, for example, had great energy but it still took him that long to receive enlightenment. If you follow the Vajrayana path, it's much quicker. If you fully observe the fundamental practice of keeping the tantric vows and *samayas*, or pledges, purely, the practice of Vajrayana can lead you to enlightenment in one or perhaps sixteen lifetimes. It's like the difference between going somewhere by airplane or train. The tantric path is like a plane; the Paramitayana path is like a train.

There are two types of realization, or *siddhi*, involved. There are the general realizations, of which there are eight—such as the attainment of the sword, the attainment of the eye medicine[58] and so forth—and the sublime realization, which is enlightenment itself. The foundation for attaining these two realizations is perfect observation of the vows and pledges, as Lama Tsongkhapa makes clear in the next verse:

> At that time, the basis of accomplishing the two attainments
> Is keeping pure vows and samaya.
> As I have become firmly convinced of this,
> Please bless me to protect these vows and pledges like my life.

He says "Please bless me to observe the vows and pledges just as I take care of my life" because he thinks that in order to receive the "uncreated," or effortless, stage, it is more important to observe the

---

[58] See Khunu Lama Rinpoche's commentary to *Lamp for the Path*, p. 17.

vows and pledges, the foundation of all realizations, than to take care of the temporal life.

The next verse alludes to the four classes of tantra—the Kriya, Charya, Yoga and Maha-anuttara tantras.[59]

> Then, having realized the importance of the two stages,
> The essence of the Vajrayana,
> By practicing with great energy, never giving up the four
>   sessions,
> Please bless me to realize the teachings of the holy guru.

The main form of tantra that we should practice is Highest Yoga Tantra, which includes father tantras, such as Yamantaka, and mother tantras, such as Heruka and Kalachakra. This class of tantra also includes the graduated paths of generation (kye-rim) and completion (dzog-rim) stages. One tantric teaching likens these two stages to a flower and its smell. Without the flower, there's no smell of the flower; similarly, without the generation stage, there's no way to practice the completion stage.

There are different ways of dividing up the day into sessions, like four sessions of six hours each, two in the day and two in the night, or six sessions of four hours each, three in the day and three in the night.

The next verse reads,

> Like that, may the gurus who show the noble path
> And the spiritual friends who practice it have long lives.
> Please bless me to pacify completely
> All outer and inner hindrances.

Here we pray for blessings for our gurus, who show us the noble path, and our spiritual friends, who follow it correctly, to live long

[59] Action, Performance, Yoga and Highest Yoga Tantras.

lives, and for ourselves to be able to pacify outer and inner hindrances. Outer hindrances are, for example, external enemies—other living beings who harm us and disturb our Dharma practice. Inner hindrances are such things as the sicknesses that afflict our body and negativities that afflict our mind. We ask for blessings to pacify all those hindrances.

The last verse says,

In all my lives, never separated from perfect gurus,
May I enjoy the magnificent Dharma.
By completing the qualities of the stages and paths,
May I quickly attain the state of Vajradhara.

We pray that in all future lives may we never be separated from perfect gurus, because the guru is the root of the path. Even though there's benefit in simply meeting a guru, the actual purpose of doing so is to practice; therefore, we pray to enjoy the Dharma through having met a guru and to follow the guru correctly in order to realize the grounds and paths and thereby quickly achieve the enlightened state of Vajradhara.

That is a brief explanation of this prayer, the *Foundation of All Good Qualities*, which, although short, is a very precious teaching. It contains all the important, essential points of the path to enlightenment. I received this teaching from His Holiness the Dalai Lama in Sarnath.

. . . . .

There are five great branches of knowledge: sound, logic, hygiene, handicrafts and inner knowledge. Outer knowledge has been well developed in the West. I've also heard about Western psychology, which is the study of the mind, but although I don't know much about it, I'm sure it's not like the inner knowledge of Buddhadharma.

Also, there are other religions, like Christianity, and they also have a kind of inner knowledge, but again, it's nothing like

Buddhadharma. All the many non-Buddhist religions have their qualities, but they're not like Buddhadharma. Within Christianity you find Catholicism, Protestantism and so forth. They all have their own views, but they don't talk about view like Buddhadharma does; they don't talk about ultimate nature, reality.

Non-Buddhist religions do have a kind of view. They believe in the self-existent I—but this is precisely what we need to abandon. According to Buddhadharma, the self-existent I is the wrong conception that we're supposed to get rid of.

People in the West aren't too concerned about future lives. However, I'm not just saying that Christianity is bad and Buddhism is good. If you study religion you'll come to your own conclusion. Through your own experience you'll prove to yourself that Buddhism is correct and other teachings are not; you'll prove to yourself what's right and what's wrong.

Within Buddhadharma itself, there are the four types of different doctrine that I mentioned at the beginning: Vaibhashika, Sautrantika, Cittamatra and Madhyamaka. The view of the Sautrantikas negates that of the Vaibhashikas, the view of the Cittamatrins negates that of the Sautrantikas, and the view of the Madhyamikas negates that of the Cittamatrins. Thus, even within Buddhadharma, there are four doctrines whose views differ from each other. In other words, as long as a view is imperfect, it can always be negated, or contradicted, by one that is more correct.

Of the five great branches of knowledge, what you should study is the fifth—inner knowledge; Buddhadharma. It is very good, very pleasing, that you have come from the West to study Buddhadharma at Kopan Monastery. The teaching of the Buddha is the method whereby you can benefit all sentient beings. Therefore you should study it well and then, like the shining sun, spread it in the West.

The Dharma that came from India to Tibet contains both sutra and tantra. If you really want to understand all these teachings, you have to become fluent in the Tibetan language, its vocabulary, grammar and so forth.

Guru Shakyamuni Buddha received enlightenment through reciting the mantra TADYATHA OM MUNÉ MUNÉ MAHAMUNAYE SOHA.[60] Therefore, you too should recite it continuously. Say it twenty-one times with the TADYATHA at the beginning, then continue reciting without it, as many times as you can. Reciting this mantra once purifies 80,000 eons' worth of negative karma. This is a very powerful mantra.

I don't have anything material to offer you to take back to the West as gifts for your family and friends but there is one thing that I can give you—this mantra. This is the one thing I can give you to take back to people in the West. In other words, you should teach this mantra to others.

Therefore, staying at Kopan, you should follow the guru and complete your study of Dharma. Tibetan Buddhism contains great inner knowledge, the best inner knowledge. By living at Kopan, you should complete your study of Buddhadharma, inner knowledge. The more you study Dharma, the deeper it becomes; it gets more and more profound. The more you study other subjects, the lighter they become.

Lama Tsongkhapa wrote several lam-rim texts, such as the *Great Treatise on the Steps of the Path to Enlightenment* (*Lam-rim Chen-mo*), the *Middle-length Lam-rim* (*Lam-rim Dring*) and the most abbreviated version, *A Concise Exposition* (*Lam-rim Dü-dön* or *Lam-rim Nyam-gur*), sometimes also called *Lines of Experience.*[61] The subject matter contained in the *Great Treatise* is explained in the intermediate version and the subject matter contained in the intermediate version is explained in the most concise one, the *Lam-rim Dü-dön*. All these teachings are condensed in Lama Tsongkhapa's

---

[60] This is as close as we can get to the way Khunu Lama Rinpoche told us to pronounce the mantra. He was clear that this is the right way.

[61] The *Great Treatise* has been published by Snow Lion; a translation of the *Middle-Length Lam-rim* is available from the FPMT; for *Lines of Experience*, see the Dalai Lama, *Illuminating the Path*, appendix 2.

letter to his disciple, the *Three Principal Aspects of the Path*. The teaching I have explained today, the *Foundation of All Good Qualities*, is a short lam-rim teaching in the form of a prayer.

Do you have any questions?

Q. When I study, especially emptiness, I think I understand something correctly and keep going in that direction but later on I see that my understanding was wrong and I wasted time following it. By going off on these tangents, I prevent myself from progressing more quickly in the right direction. How can I relate to the experiences I have in such a way that I don't waste time exploring what turn out to be wrong conceptions?

Khunu Lama Rinpoche. First, I can see that you are all trying to do great, extensive Dharma work, and I will pray for you to be successful and benefit the teaching of the Buddha. With respect to your question, when you are studying or meditating on emptiness, it is possible for fear to arise or for you to realize that what you have always believed to be true is wrong. However, fundamentally, what your mind should be avoiding is the two extremes of self-existence and non-existence. Your pure view of emptiness should be devoid of these two extremes; it should be in the middle way. Then your view of emptiness is correct. Even the conception holding emptiness is empty.

Q. I have a question about conventional truth. There are false conventional truth and right conventional truth. Is it possible for a person who has the wrong conception of the self-existent I to ever perceive right conventional truth? There are two ways in which a person can view something: as something there or as something not there. For example, a person looking at tsampa can see it as free from dirt or as contaminated. There are two different ways of seeing it. As long as the person has the wrong conception of self-existence, does that prevent her from having the right conventional view, from perceiving right conventional truth?

Khunu Lama Rinpoche. What is the right conventional truth of tsampa? When everybody looks at the tsampa, they see tsampa. Not only that, tsampa has to be viewed through intact senses; senses that are not defective. It is right conventional truth if it exists as an object of normal senses. Also, when other people look at the tsampa, they see tsampa. That is what we recognize as right conventional truth.

For example, when you're in a moving train, the trees also seem to be moving. Sometimes you get this kind of wrong conception. Or when a conjurer transforms inanimate objects, like pieces of wood, so that they appear in the form of animals, or when you see a white conch shell as yellow, those are wrong conventional truths because they are a projection of defective senses. Also, it's proven that they're wrong because they are not seen as that by other worldly beings, those who have not realized emptiness.

Finally, according to the Madhyamaka scriptures, the I that non-Buddhist philosophers believe to be self-existent is also a wrong conventional truth.

Q. Please could you explain the difference between conventional and ultimate bodhicitta?

Khunu Lama Rinpoche. Ultimate bodhicitta, the realization of fully seeing ultimate nature as the Madhyamaka teachings explain, is achieved on the first of the ten bodhisattva grounds.

Conventional bodhicitta is explained in Shantideva's *Guide to the Bodhisattva's Way of Life.* There are two types of conventional bodhicitta—aspirational and engaging. Aspirational bodhicitta is the wish to attain enlightenment for the sake of all sentient beings; engaging bodhicitta is actually following the path to enlightenment.

Even worldly people, those who have not attained the path of seeing, can achieve aspirational bodhicitta. As you know, there are five paths—the paths of merit, preparation, right-seeing, meditation and no more learning. Even those on the first of these five paths can achieve conventional bodhicitta. The two types of conventional bodhicitta have been explained in Shantideva's *Guide,* and ultimate bodhicitta has been explained by Nagarjuna and also in certain tantras. Ultimate bodhicitta is actually ultimate nature.

However, since bodhicitta is the seed of buddhahood, like the seed of a plant, it's the main thing we need to develop in our mind. Bodhicitta is what we should strive our hardest to achieve. The Buddha himself said that all the buddhas come from bodhicitta.

Q. Many of us will soon be going back to the West. Since you mentioned that we should take the Dharma back with us, what's the best way to present it?

Khunu Lama Rinpoche. You should try to teach the Dharma according to what suits the minds of those listening to you. If explaining ultimate nature is appropriate, you can follow the brief explanation in Lama Tsongkhapa's *Three Principal Aspects* or the more elaborate one in his *Great Treatise,* which has more than one hundred pages on emptiness. If you want to explain the method side of the teachings, you can do so according to Shantideva's *Guide,* where he talks about the practice of the first five perfections of generosity, morality, patience, effort and concentration. You can also explain right view on the basis of [the ninth chapter of] the *Guide,* if it fits the minds of your listeners.[62] In short, you should teach Dharma in the way that a doctor prescribes medicine. But even if the doctor has the perfect medicine for a patient's illness, he can't force the patient to take it. That's an unskillful approach. The wise doctor treats patients according to their capacity. Dharma should be presented in the same way.

Q. Our mind is always discriminating things like "I like him, I don't like her" and we're usually so unconscious that we're totally unaware that we're doing this. Now I'm starting to realize that dis-

criminating in this way causes suffering. Since developing equanimity is the first step to bodhicitta, how can we equalize our mind in
our everyday situations to avoid discriminating between the people
we like and those we don't?

Khunu Lama Rinpoche. You should check in the following way.
If there's an outer object that you think is good, bad or ugly, try to
see its ultimate nature by analyzing every atom. Mentally reduce
the object you see as good to atoms, take even the atoms apart and,
analyzing it like this, try to see its emptiness. Again, analyze the
object you see as ugly down to its atoms, analyze even the atoms,
and, in this way, try to see its emptiness. When you do this, you'll
see there's absolutely no difference between these two objects. In
your conventional view you discriminate them as different, but in
emptiness, you don't.

Q. How can we unite these two views—the conventional with the
ultimate?

Khunu Lama Rinpoche. The mere appearance of an object is the
conventional view. That should be seen as illusory but at the same
time unified with emptiness. The conventional view should be one
with emptiness. But that doesn't mean that your view of an object
that you believe to be truly existent is really true. This view and
the view that sees the object as illusory and empty cannot become
one. This is very difficult to realize. Therefore, it is important that
you get as clear an intellectual understanding of it as possible. First,
understand how things are dependent upon causes and conditions;
you must understand the born and the unborn, in other words,
dependent phenomena and emptiness respectively.

Q. Rinpoche, you said that we should teach people according to
their level of mind. How can we discern this? Do we have enough
wisdom to know if it is appropriate to teach mantras, visualizations
and so forth to interested Western people?

Khunu Lama Rinpoche. That is hard to answer specifically but what you can teach is this. Visualize a white cloud in the space in front of you at the level of your forehead. On that is a large throne upon which is seated Guru Shakyamuni Buddha in his usual aspect of a monk adorned with robes, with his right hand over his knee touching the moon cushion and his left in the meditation mudra. He is surrounded on all sides by countless buddhas, bodhisattvas, such as the eight great bodhisattvas, and arhats.

Powerful light rays emanate from Guru Shakyamuni Buddha and the others and enter you and all other sentient beings, who appear in human form surrounding you, purifying all the negativities accumulated since beginningless time and bringing all the realizations of the graduated path to enlightenment. While visualizing this, recite Guru Shakyamuni Buddha's mantra, TADYATHA OM MUNÉ MUNÉ MAHAMUNAYE SOHA or OM MUNÉ MUNÉ MAHAMUNAYE SOHA, as I mentioned before. No matter which of these two versions you recite, the visualization is the same.

Then make a strong decision in your mind that through this purification, you and all other sentient beings have become irreversible bodhisattvas, thus pleasing the infinite buddhas.

· · · · ·

From my side, I will pray for you never to be separated from the guru in all future lifetimes, to complete the path and attain enlightenment as quickly as possible. I will pray for you to accomplish the entire Dharma and to have long lives in order for this to happen. It is not sufficient for just me to have a long life, as you have requested. You, too, should try to live long. So, I will pray for that, but my prayers alone will not be enough; from your side, you also have to try.

The great bodhisattva Khunu Lama Rinpoche gave this teaching to the monks and nuns of the International Mahayana Institute in Boudhanath, Nepal, 14 February 1975. It was translated by Lama Zopa Rinpoche.

Various Aspects of Tantra

His Holiness Trijang Rinpoche

FRED VON ALLMEN

THE RELATIONSHIP BETWEEN BUDDHIST AND HINDU TANTRA

ALTHOUGH SOME SCHOLARS have maintained that Buddhist tantra was derived from Hinduism, this is not correct. This theory, prevalent among those who adhere to the tenets of the Hinayana, is based on a superficial resemblance of various elements of the two systems, such as the forms of the deities, the meditations on psychic channels and winds, the fire rituals and so forth. Though certain practices, like the repetition of mantras, are common to both the Hindu and Buddhist tantric traditions, their interpretation—their inner meaning—is vastly different. Furthermore, Buddhist tantra is superior because, unlike Hinduism, it contains the three principal aspects of the path: renunciation, bodhicitta and the right view of emptiness.

As even animals want freedom from suffering, there are non-Buddhist practitioners who want to be free from contaminated feelings of happiness and therefore cultivate the preparatory state of the fourth meditative absorption. There are even some non-Buddhist meditators who temporarily renounce contaminated feelings of happiness and attain levels higher than the four absorptions.[63] However, only Buddhists renounce all of these as well as neutral feelings and pervasive compounding suffering. Then, by meditating on the sufferings together with their causes, the mental defilements, they can be abandoned forever. This explains why, even though non-Buddhists meditate on the form and formless states and attain the peak of worldly existence, they cannot abandon the mental defilements of this state. Therefore, when they meet with the right

---

[63] For details of the concentrations and the formless absorptions, see Lati Rinbochay and Denma Lochö Rinbochay. *Meditative States in Tibetan Buddhism.*

circumstances, anger and the other delusions manifest, karma is created and they remain in cyclic existence.

Because of this and similar reasons, such practices are not fit to be included in the Mahayana. They resemble neither the practices of the common sutra path—which comprises renunciation, yearning for freedom from the whole of cyclic existence; the wisdom correctly understanding emptiness, the right view, which is the antidote to ignorance, the root of cyclic existence; and bodhicitta, the mind determined to reach enlightenment for the sake of all sentient beings—nor those of the exclusive Buddhist tantric path of the Great Vehicle.

THE ORIGIN OF TANTRA

The tantras were taught by the Buddha himself in the form of his supreme manifestation as a monk, as the great Vajradhara and in various manifestations of the central deity of specific mandalas. The great beings Manjushri, Samantabhadra, Vajrapani and others, urged by the Buddha, also taught some tantras.

In terms of the four classes of tantra, the Kriya tantras were taught by the Buddha in the form of a monk in the Heaven of Thirty-three on the summit of Mt. Meru and in the human world, where Manjushri and others were the chief hearers. The tantras requested by the bodhisattva Pungzang were taught in the realm of Vajrapani. Others were taught by the Buddha himself and, with his blessings, Avalokiteshvara, Manjushri and Vajrapani. There were also some that were spoken by worldly gods.

The Charya tantras were taught by the Buddha in the form of his supreme manifestation in the celestial realms and in the realm called Base and Essence Adorned with Flowers.

The Yoga tantras were taught by the Buddha when he arose in the form of the central deity of each mandala in such places as the summit of Mt. Meru and in the fifth celestial realm of desire.

The Anuttara tantras were also taught by the Buddha. In the

land of Ögyan, having manifested the mandala of Guhyasamaja, he taught this tantra to King Indrabodhi. At the time of the subduing of the demonic forces, the Buddha taught the Yamantaka tantras when they were requested by either the consort of Yamantaka or the consort of Kalachakra. He taught the Hevajra tantra when he arose in the form of Hevajra in the land of Magadha at the time of destroying the four maras; it was requested by Vajragarbha and the consort of Hevajra. Having been requested by Vajrayogini, the Buddha manifested as Heruka and taught the root tantra of Heruka on the summit of Mt. Meru, and when requested by Vajrapani, taught the explanatory tantra. As for the Kalachakra tantra, which was requested by King Suchandra, a manifestation of Vajrapani, the mighty Buddha went to the glorious shrine of Dhanyakataka in south India and, manifesting the mandala of the *dharmadhatu*[64] speech surmounted by the mandala of Kalachakra, taught it there.

Although he appeared in many different manifestations, the tantras were actually taught by the enlightened teacher, Lord Buddha.

WHAT HAPPENS DURING AN INITIATION

There are many differences, some great and some small, in the initiations of each of the four classes of tantra. Therefore, one initiation is not sufficient for all mandalas. When receiving an initiation from a qualified master, certain fortunate and qualified disciples develop the wisdom of the initiation in their mindstreams. Otherwise, sitting in on an initiation, experiencing the vase, water and other initiations, will plant imprints to listen to Dharma in your mind but not much else will happen. Still, you need an initiation if you want to study tantra. If the secrets of tantra are explained to somebody who has not received an initiation, the guru commits the seventh tantric

[64] Tib: *chö-ying*. Literally, "the essence or expanse of phenomena." All-encompassing space. Can be synonymous with buddha nature.

root downfall and the explanation is of no benefit whatsoever to the disciple.

THE RELATIONSHIP BETWEEN SUTRA AND TANTRA

Regarding renunciation and bodhicitta, there is no difference between Sutrayana and Tantrayana, but regarding conduct there is. Three kinds of conduct have been taught: disciples who admire and have faith in the Hinayana should separate themselves from all desires; disciples who admire the Sutrayana should traverse the stages and practice the perfections; those who admire the deep teachings of the Tantrayana should work with the conduct of the path of desire.

From the point of view of the philosophy, there is no difference in emptiness as an object of cognition but there is a difference in the method of its realization. In the sutra tradition, the conscious mind engages in meditative equipoise on emptiness; in tantra, the innate wisdom, an extremely subtle mind, is involved—the difference, therefore, is great. The main practice of Sutrayana, engaging in the path as a cause to achieve the form and wisdom bodies of a buddha, is the accumulation of wisdom and merit for three countless eons and the accomplishment of one's own buddha fields. Therefore, Sutrayana is known as the causal vehicle.

In tantra, even when still a beginner, one concentrates and meditates on the four complete purities that are similar to the result—the completely pure body, pure realm, pure possessions and pure deeds of an enlightened being. Thus, tantra is known as the resultant vehicle.

THE FOUR TRADITIONS

With respect to sutra, the explanation of the Hinayana and Mahayana is the same in all the four great traditions of Tibetan Buddhism. Also, as far as the preliminary practices are concerned, there are no differences apart from the names. In the Gelug tradition they are called "the stages of the path of the three scopes"; in the Kagyü they are known as "the four ways to change the mind"; in the Drikung Kagyü as "the four Dharmas of Dagpa and the five of Drikung"; and the Sakya refer to "separation from the four attachments." [Kyabje Rinpoche did not refer to the Nyingma tradition here.]

With respect to tantra, the individual master's way of leading the disciples on the path depends on his experience and the instructions of the root texts and the commentaries of the great practitioners. Accordingly, the entrance into practice is taught a little differently. However, all are the same in that they lead to the final attainment of the state of Vajradhara.

Bio 16

Kyabje Trijang Rinpoche (1901–81), the late junior tutor of His Holiness the Dalai Lama, was also the root guru of Lama Yeshe, Lama Zopa Rinpoche, Geshe Rabten, Geshe Dhargyey and many other great twentieth-century teachers of the Gelug tradition. He was the main disciple of Pabongka Rinpoche and editor of *Liberation in the Palm of Your Hand*. The above excerpts from a teaching given to Western Dharma students in Dharamsala were first published in *From Tushita* in 1977. Translated by Gavin Kilty.

Appendix 1
Developing Equanimity:
The Mahayana Equilibrium Meditation

Lama Zopa Rinpoche

Meditate in the first person and pause for contemplation between paragraphs.

Think: It is never enough to gain only self-liberation. Attachment to personal peace and striving solely for this is both selfish and cruel.

Visualize that you are surrounded by all sentient beings, with your mother seated to your left and your father to your right. In front of you, visualize an enemy; somebody who dislikes you or wishes you harm. Behind you, place your dearest friend; the person to whom you are most attached. To the side, visualize a stranger; somebody for whom your feelings are neutral.

Think: There is no reason at all for me to be attached to and help my friend or to hate and harm my enemy.

If I were to strive for only my own peace, there would be no reason for me to have been born human. Even as an animal, I could strive for this. The various animals have the same aim as many highly educated people—self-happiness—and also create many negative actions, such as fighting with and destroying enemies, cheating others and so forth, all in the pursuit of their own happiness. There is almost no difference between them and us except their shape.

The main purpose of my having been born human is to strive for and achieve higher aims—to bring every sentient being to everlasting happiness. This is something no animal can ever do.

Just as I wish to avoid suffering and find happiness, so, too, do all other sentient beings. Therefore, I and all other sentient beings are equal, and there is no logical reason for me to care more about myself than others or to harm enemies or any other sentient being.

For countless rebirths I have been discriminating between other beings as friend, enemy or stranger with the self-I consciousness. Chandrakirti said, "Where there is self-I consciousness, there is discrimination of 'other.'" From partisanship that discriminates between self and other, attachment and hatred arise.

All misfortune arises from acting under the influence of these negative minds. The self-I consciousness causes attachment to self, which produces attachment to my own happiness.

The self-I consciousness causes attachment to self, which produces attachment to my own happiness.

The entire range of negative minds arises from the above. Anger is caused by greed and self-attachment and makes me discriminate against whoever disturbs my happiness, producing the enemy. Attachment creates the friend, who helps, and determines the enemy, who hinders. Ignorance labels those who neither help nor hinder as strangers.

Anger makes me hate and harm the enemy; attachment makes me cling to and help the friend; and ignorance makes me see the stranger as having a permanent nature. By acting under the influence of these negative minds, I lead myself into difficult and suffering situations.

Attachment creates danger and suffering for myself and others. The whole earth is in danger of exploding. Attachment offers no peace and brings only suffering.

Since beginningless time, the two negative actions of helping out of attachment and harming out of anger have thrown me into samsaric suffering, making it impossible for me to achieve the perfect peace of liberation and enlightenment.

Negative actions leave negative imprints on the consciousness; these ripen into endless experiences of suffering. If I continue to behave in this way, I will experience the same suffering over and over again for eons and will never receive any realizations, let alone enlightenment.

The three objects of friend, enemy and stranger are false and have been labeled incorrectly for extremely temporal reasons. The current friend, enemy and stranger have not always been friend, enemy and stranger in my countless, previous lives. Even the enemy of last year can this year become my friend and yesterday's friend can become my enemy today. It can all change within an hour and does so because of attachment to things like food, clothing and reputation.

A scripture says, "If you try for a moment to befriend an enemy, he will become your friend. The opposite occurs if you treat a friend like an enemy. Therefore, the wise, understanding the impermanent nature of temporal relationships, are never attached to food, clothing or reputation."

Lord Buddha said, "In another life, the father becomes the son; the mother, the wife; the enemy, a friend. It always changes. In cyclic existence, nothing is certain."

Therefore, there is no reason to be attached to friends or to hate enemies.

If the ignorant, self-I conception and its objects were true, the three designations of friend, enemy and stranger should have existed from countless previous lives and should continue to exist through the present to beyond enlightenment. This would make complete nonsense of the concept of enlightenment, since the Buddha's sublime, enlightened mind is completely free of the delusions and imprints that create such distinctions.

Out of his compassion, Lord Buddha taught the equilibrium meditation so that I, too, might become free of delusions, imprints and ignorant discrimination. The concepts of friend, enemy and stranger are false because they and their basis are totally illusory. There is no self-I.

My problems are created not by the enemy but by me. In my previous lives, I harmed others through ignorance and the results of this have returned in this life, causing me hardship and suffering.

Lord Buddha said, "In previous lives, I have killed all of you before and you have all slaughtered me. Why should we now be attached to each other?"

Chandrakirti said, "It is foolish and ignorant to retaliate to an enemy's attack with spite in hopes of ending it, as the retaliation itself only brings more suffering."

Therefore, there is no reason to retaliate.

The enemy is the object of my practice of patience, which helps me overcome my anger. I should not hate this enemy, who brings peace into my mind.

The enemy is infinitely more precious than any material possession. He is the source of all my past, present and future happiness. I should never hate the enemy. Any possession can be given up for his peace.

An enemy is my greatest need, the source of all beings' enlightenment, including my own. The enemy is my most precious possession. For his peace I can give up myself.

The enemy harming me mentally and physically is under the control of his negative mind. He is like the stick that somebody uses to beat another. There is no reason to get angry or to retaliate by harming the enemy. It is not his fault; just as the pain I experience from a beating is not the fault of the stick. From now on I must never hate or harm the enemy or any other being.

If I had clear wisdom I would see that harming others out of hatred is harming myself out of hatred. Obviously, I should not harm others.

All sentient beings, including the enemy, are the object of Lord Buddha's compassion. The numberless buddhas hold the enemy and all other beings dear to their heart. Therefore, harming another, even slightly, is like harming the infinite buddhas.

The Buddha always considers all sentient beings, including enemies, to be more important than himself. Mindlessly harming another being for my own benefit is the act of a mind of stone.

The enemy and all other sentient beings have been my mother countless times. The holy body, speech and mind of the infinite buddhas are servant to all beings, enemies included. Therefore, I must never give harm to any other being.

My worst enemy is the ignorance in my own mind. Destroying an outer enemy instead of my own ignorance is like killing a friend by mistaking him for an enemy. I should not harm the outer enemy but the inner one, the actual cause of all my suffering.

Because of transcendent realizations based on the equilibrium meditation, no bodhisattva would ever see another sentient being as an enemy, even if all rose against him or her.

The enemy is merely a concept created by my hatred, just as friends and strangers are concepts created by my attachment and ignorance. I should not believe the distorted perceptions of my negative minds.

If I investigate with my wisdom eye, I will never find my attachment's friend or my hatred's enemy anywhere, neither inside nor outside their bodies. Wisdom tells me that these are merely names.

For all these reasons, I can now clearly see how foolish and nonsensical I have been over beginningless lifetimes.

If you could realize this equilibrium meditation it would be your most priceless possession. Equilibrium brings peace to numberless beings and all your future lives.

Colophon

This meditation comes from Lama Zopa Rinpoche's book, *The Wish-fulfilling Golden Sun of the Mahayana Thought Training*, Kopan Monastery, 1974. Find it at LamaYeshe.com. Rinpoche has described it as more than the standard equilibrium meditation as he has added a number of techniques for overcoming anger and developing patience.

APPENDIX 2
A LAMP FOR THE PATH TO ENLIGHTENMENT
by Atisha Dipamkara Shrijnana (982-1054)[65]

Homage to the bodhisattva, the youthful Manjushri.

1. I pay homage with great respect
To the conquerors of the three times,
To their teaching and to those who aspire to virtue.
Urged by the good disciple Jangchub Ö
I shall illuminate the lamp
For the path to enlightenment.

2. Understand that there are three kinds of persons
Because of their small, middling and supreme capacities.
I shall write clearly distinguishing
Their individual characteristics.

3. Know that those who by whatever means
Seek for themselves no more
Than the pleasures of cyclic existence
Are persons of the least capacity.

4. Those who seek peace for themselves alone,
Turning away from worldly pleasures

[65] With thanks to Shambhala Publications for permission to use Ruth Sonam's excellent translation in this book. See *Atisha's Lamp for the Path to Enlightenment* for Geshe Sonam Rinchen's commentary. For the Dalai Lama's commentary, see *Illuminating the Path*.

And avoiding destructive actions
Are said to be of middling capacity.

5. Those who, through their personal suffering,
Truly want to end completely
All the suffering of others
Are persons of supreme capacity.

6. For those excellent living beings,
Who desire supreme enlightenment,
I shall explain the perfect methods
Taught by the spiritual teachers.

7. Facing paintings, statues and so forth
Of the completely enlightened one,
Reliquaries and the excellent teaching,
Offer flowers, incense—whatever you have.

8. With the seven-part offering
From the *[Prayer of] Noble Conduct*,
With the thought never to turn back
Till you gain ultimate enlightenment,

9. And with strong faith in the Three Jewels,
Kneeling with one knee on the ground
And your hands pressed together,
First of all take refuge three times.

10. Next, beginning with an attitude
Of love for all living creatures,
Consider beings, excluding none,
Suffering in the three bad rebirths,
Suffering birth, death and so forth.

11. Then, since you want to free these beings
From the suffering of pain,
From suffering and the cause of suffering,
Arouse immutably the resolve
To attain enlightenment.

12. The qualities of developing
Such an aspiration are
Fully explained by Maitreya
In the *Array of Trunks Sutra*.

13. Having learned about the infinite benefits
Of the intention to gain full enlightenment
By reading this sutra or listening to a teacher,
Arouse it repeatedly to make it steadfast.

14. The *Sutra Requested by Viradatta*
Fully explains the merit therein.
At this point, in summary,
I will cite just three verses.

15. If it possessed physical form,
The merit of the altruistic intention
Would completely fill the whole of space
And exceed even that.

16. If someone were to fill with jewels
As many buddha fields as there are grains
Of sand in the Ganges
To offer to the Protector of the World,

17. This would be surpassed by
The gift of folding one's hands

And inclining one's mind to enlightenment,
For such is limitless.

18. Having developed the aspiration for enlightenment,
Constantly enhance it through concerted effort.
To remember it in this and also in other lives,
Keep the precepts properly as explained.

19. Without the vow of the engaged intention,
Perfect aspiration will not grow.
Make effort definitely to take it,
Since you want the wish for enlightenment to grow.

20. Those who maintain any of the seven kinds
Of individual liberation vow
Have the ideal [prerequisite] for
The bodhisattva vow, not others.

21. The Tathagata spoke of seven kinds
Of individual liberation vow.
The best of these is glorious pure conduct,
Said to be the vow of a fully ordained person.

22. According to the ritual described in
The chapter on discipline in the *Bodhisattva Stages*,
Take the vow from a good
And well-qualified spiritual teacher.

23. Understand that a good spiritual teacher
Is one skilled in the vow ceremony,
Who lives by the vow and has
The confidence and compassion to bestow it.

24. However, in case you try but cannot
Find such a spiritual teacher,
I shall explain another
Correct procedure for taking the vow.

25. I shall write here very clearly, as explained
In the *Ornament of Manjushri's Buddha Land Sutra*,
How, long ago, when Manjushri was Ambaraja,
He aroused the intention to become enlightened.

26. "In the presence of the protectors,
I arouse the intention to gain full enlightenment.
I invite all beings as my guests
And shall free them from cyclic existence.

27. "From this moment onwards
Until I attain enlightenment,
I shall not harbor harmful thoughts,
Anger, avarice or envy.

28. "I shall cultivate pure conduct,
Give up wrong-doing and desire
And with joy in the vow of discipline
Train myself to follow the buddhas.

29. "I shall not be eager to reach
Enlightenment in the quickest way,
But shall stay behind till the very end,
For the sake of a single being.

30. "I shall purify limitless
Inconceivable lands
And remain in the ten directions
For all those who call my name.

31. "I shall purify all my bodily
And verbal forms of activity.
My mental activities, too, I shall purify
And do nothing that is non-virtuous."

32. When those observing the vow
Of the active altruistic intention have trained well
In the three forms of discipline, their respect
For these three forms of discipline grows,
Which causes purity of body, speech and mind.

33. Therefore, through effort in the vow made by
Bodhisattvas for pure, full enlightenment,
The collections for complete enlightenment
Will be thoroughly accomplished.

34. All buddhas say the cause for the completion
Of the collections, whose nature is
Merit and exalted wisdom,
Is the development of higher perception.

35. Just as a bird with undeveloped
Wings cannot fly in the sky,
Those without the power of higher perception
Cannot work for the good of living beings.

36. The merit gained in a single day
By one who possesses higher perception
Cannot be gained even in a hundred lifetimes
By one without such higher perception.

37. Those who want swiftly to complete
The collections for full enlightenment

Will accomplish higher perception
Through effort, not through laziness.

38. Without the attainment of calm abiding,
Higher perception will not occur.
Therefore make repeated effort
To accomplish calm abiding.

39. While the conditions for calm abiding
Are incomplete, meditative stabilization
Will not be accomplished, even if one meditates
Strenuously for thousands of years.

40. Thus maintaining well the conditions mentioned
In the *Collection for Meditative Stabilization Chapter*,
Place the mind on any one
Virtuous focal object.

41. When the practitioner has gained calm abiding,
Higher perception will also be gained,
But without practice of the perfection of wisdom,
The obstructions will not come to an end.

42. Thus, to eliminate all obstructions
To liberation and omniscience,
The practitioner should continually cultivate
The perfection of wisdom with skillful means.

43. Wisdom without skillful means
And skillful means, too, without wisdom
Are referred to as bondage.
Therefore do not give up either.

44. To eliminate doubts concerning
What is called wisdom and what skillful means,
I shall make clear the difference
Between skillful means and wisdom.

45. Apart from the perfection of wisdom,
All virtuous practices such as
The perfection of giving are described
As skillful means by the Victorious Ones.

46. Whoever, under the influence of familiarity
With skillful means, cultivates wisdom
Will quickly attain enlightenment—
Not just by meditating on selflessness.

47. Understanding emptiness of inherent existence
Through realizing that the aggregates, constituents
And sources are not produced
Is described as wisdom.

48. Something existent cannot be produced,
Nor something non-existent, like a sky flower.
These errors are both absurd and thus
Both of the two will not occur either.

49. A thing is not produced from itself,
Nor from another, also not from both,
Nor causelessly either, thus it does not
Exist inherently by way of its own entity.

50. Moreover, when all phenomena are examined
As to whether they are one or many,
They are not seen to exist by way of their own entity,
And thus are ascertained as not inherently existent.

51. The reasoning of the *Seventy Stanzas on Emptiness*,
The *Treatise on the Middle Way* and so forth
Explain that the nature of all things
Is established as emptiness.

52. Since there are a great many passages,
I have not cited them here,
But have explained just their conclusions
For the purpose of meditation.

53. Thus, whatever is meditation
On selflessness, in that it does not observe
An inherent nature in phenomena,
Is the cultivation of wisdom.

54. Just as wisdom does not see
An inherent nature in phenomena,
Having analyzed wisdom itself by reasoning,
Non-conceptually meditate on that.

55. The nature of this worldly existence,
Which has come from conceptualization,
Is conceptuality. Thus the elimination of
Conceptuality is the highest state of nirvana.

56. The great ignorance of conceptuality
Makes us fall into the ocean of cyclic existence.
Resting in non-conceptual stabilization,
Space-like non-conceptuality manifests clearly.

57. When bodhisattvas non-conceptually contemplate
This excellent teaching, they will transcend
Conceptuality, so hard to overcome,
And eventually reach the non-conceptual state.

58. Having ascertained through scripture
And through reasoning that phenomena
Are not produced nor inherently existent,
Meditate without conceptuality.

59. Having thus meditated on suchness,
Eventually, after reaching "heat" and so forth,
The "very joyful" and the others are attained
And, before long, the enlightened state of buddhahood.

60. If you wish to create with ease
The collections for enlightenment
Through activities of pacification,
Increase and so forth, gained by the power of mantra,

61. And also through the force of the eight
And other great attainments like the "good pot"—
If you want to practice secret mantra,
As explained in the action and performance tantras,

62. Then, to receive the preceptor initiation,
You must please an excellent spiritual teacher
Through service, valuable gifts and the like
As well as through obedience.

63. Through the full bestowing of the preceptor initiation,
By a spiritual teacher who is pleased,
You are purified of all wrong-doing
And become fit to gain powerful attainments.

64. Because the *Great Tantra of the Primordial Buddha*
Forbids it emphatically,
Those observing pure conduct should not
Take the secret and wisdom initiations.

65. If those observing the austere practice of pure conduct
Were to hold these initiations,
Their vow of austerity would be impaired
Through doing that which is proscribed.

66. This creates transgressions that are a defeat
For those observing discipline.
Since they are certain to fall to a bad rebirth,
They will never gain accomplishments.

67. There is no fault if one who has received
The preceptor initiation and has knowledge
Of suchness listens to or explains the tantras
And performs burnt offering rituals,
Or makes offering of gifts and so forth.

68. I, the Elder Dipamkarashri, having seen it
Explained in sutra and in other teachings,
Have made this concise explanation
At the request of Jangchub Ö.

Colophon
This concludes *A Lamp for the Path to Enlightenment*, by the Acharya Dipamkara Shrijnana. It was translated, revised and finalized by the eminent Indian abbot himself and by the great reviser, translator and fully ordained monk Geway Lodrö. This teaching was written in the temple of Thöling in Zhang Zhung.

Translated by Ruth Sonam, Dharamsala, January 1997.

APPENDIX 3
THE EIGHT VERSES OF THOUGHT TRANSFORMATION

1. Determined to obtain the greatest possible benefit from all sentient beings, who are more precious than a wish-fulfilling jewel, I shall hold them most dear at all times.

2. When in the company of others, I shall always consider myself the lowest of all, and from the depths of my heart hold others dear and supreme.

3. Vigilant, the moment a delusion appears in my mind, endangering myself and others, I shall confront and avert it without delay.

4. Whenever I see beings who are wicked in nature and overwhelmed by violent negative actions and suffering, I shall hold such rare ones dear, as if I had found a precious treasure.

5. When, out of envy, others mistreat me with abuse, insults or the like, I shall accept defeat and offer the victory to others.

6. When somebody whom I have benefited and in whom I have great hopes gives me terrible harm, I shall regard that person as my holy guru.

7. In short, both directly and indirectly, I offer every happiness and benefit to all my mothers. I shall secretly take upon myself all their harmful actions and suffering.

8. Undefiled by the stains of the superstitions of the eight worldly concerns, may I, by perceiving all phenomena as illusory, be released from the bondage of attachment.

Colophon
Translated by Lama Zopa Rinpoche in his "Everflowing Nectar of Bodhicitta," FPMT: *Essential Buddhist Prayers, Volume 1,* 155–66.

The foundation of all good qualities is the kind and perfect,
    pure guru;
Correct devotion to him is the root of the path.
By clearly seeing this and applying great effort,
Please bless me to rely upon him with great respect.

Understanding that the precious freedom of this rebirth is
    found only once,
Is greatly meaningful and difficult to find again,
Please bless me to generate the mind that unceasingly,
Day and night, takes its essence.

This life is as impermanent as a water bubble;
Remember how quickly it decays and death comes.
After death, just like a shadow follows the body,
The results of black and white karma follow.

Finding firm and definite conviction in this,
Please bless me always to be careful
To abandon even the slightest of negativities
And accomplish all virtuous deeds.

Seeking samsaric pleasures is the door to all suffering:
They are uncertain and cannot be relied upon.
Recognizing these shortcomings,
Please bless me to generate the strong wish for the bliss
    of liberation.

Led by this pure thought,
Mindfulness, alertness and great caution arise.
The root of the teachings is keeping the *pratimoksha* vows:
Please bless me to accomplish this essential practice.

Just as I have fallen into the sea of samsara,
So have all mother migratory beings.
Bless me to see this, train in supreme bodhicitta,
And bear the responsibility of freeing migratory beings.

Even if I develop only bodhicitta,
without practicing the three types of morality
I will not achieve enlightenment.
With my clear recognition of this,
Please bless me to practice the bodhisattva vows with
    great energy.

Once I have pacified distractions to wrong objects
And correctly analyzing the meaning of reality,
Please bless me to generate quickly within my mind-stream
The unified path of calm abiding and special insight.

Having become a pure vessel by training in the general path,
Please bless me to enter
The holy gateway of the fortunate ones:
The supreme vajra vehicle.

At that time, the basis of accomplishing the two attainments
Is keeping pure vows and *samaya*.
As I have become firmly convinced of this,
Please bless me to protect these vows and pledges like my life.

Then, having realized the importance of the two stages,
The essence of the Vajrayana,

By practicing with great energy, never giving up the four
    sessions,
Please bless me to realize the teachings of the holy guru.

Like that, may the gurus who show the noble path
And the spiritual friends who practice it have long lives.
Please bless me to pacify completely
All outer and inner hindrances.

In all my lives, never separated from perfect gurus,
May I enjoy the magnificent Dharma.
By completing the qualities of the stages and paths,
May I quickly attain the state of Vajradhara.

Colophon

This lamrim prayer was written by Lama Tsongkhapa and translated by Jampäl Lhundrup. See *Essential Buddhist Prayers, Volume 1*, 137–40.

GLOSSARY

(Skt = Sanskrit; Tib = Tibetan)

affliction. See *delusion.*

aggregates. See *five aggregates.*

arhat (Skt; Tib: dra-chom-pa). Literally, foe destroyer. A person who has destroyed his or her inner enemy, the delusions, and attained liberation from cyclic existence.

arya (Skt; Tib: phag-pa). Literally, noble. One who has realized the wisdom of emptiness.

Asanga, Arya. The fourth-century Indian master who received directly from Maitreya Buddha the extensive, or method, lineage of Shakyamuni Buddha's teachings. Said to have founded the Cittamatra School of Buddhist philosophy. He is one of six great Indian scholars, known as the Six Ornaments.

Atisha Dipamkara Shrijnana (982-1054). The renowned Indian master who went to Tibet in 1042 to help in the revival of Buddhism and established the Kadam tradition. His text *Lamp for the Path to Enlightenment* was the first lam-rim text. See Chapter 2 for more information.

Avalokiteshvara (Skt; Tib: Chenrezig). The buddha of compassion. A male meditational deity embodying fully enlightened compassion.

bardo (Tib). See *intermediate state.*

bhagavan (Skt; Tib: chom-dän-dä). Epithet for a buddha; sometimes translated as Lord, Blessed One and so forth. One who has destroyed (*chom*) all defilements, possesses all qualities (*dän*) and has transcended the world (*dä*).

bhumi (Skt; Tib: sa). Ground, or level, as in the ten bodhisattva levels. See *Meditation on Emptiness,* pp. 98-109.

bhikshu (Skt; Tib: gelong). Fully-ordained monk.

bhikshuni (Skt; Tib: gelongma). Fully-ordained nun.

bodhicitta (Skt; Tib: jang-chub sem). A principal consciousness that combines the two factors of wishing to free all beings from suffering and of wishing to attain enlightenment because of that; the spontaneous altruistic mind of enlightenment can be either aspirational or engaging.

bodhisattva (Skt; Tib: jang-chub sem-pa). One who possesses bodhicitta.

bodhisattva level. See *bhumi.*

Bodhisattvayana, Bodhisattva Vehicle. See *Paramitayana.*

buddha a (Skt; Tib: sang-gye). A fully awakened being. One who has totally eliminated (Tib: *sang*) all obscurations veiling the mind and has fully developed (Tib: *gye*) all good qualities to perfection. See also *enlightenment.*

Buddhadharma (Skt). The teachings of the Buddha. See also *Dharma.*

Buddha field (Skt: buddhaksetra; Tib: sang-gye kyi-zhing). In some ways synonymous with "pure land," it can also mean any pure environment, seen as a manifestation of wisdom.

buddhahood. See enlightenment.

buddha nature. The clear light nature of mind possessed by all sentient beings; the potential for all sentient beings to become enlightened by removing the two obscurations to liberation and omniscience. See also *obscurations.*

Buddhist (Tib: nang-pa). One who has taken refuge in the Three Jewels of Refuge: Buddha, Dharma and Sangha and who accepts the philosophical world view of the "four seals": that all composite phenomena are impermanent, all contaminated phenomena are in the nature of suffering, all things and events are devoid of self-existence and nirvana is true peace.

calm abiding. See *shamatha.*

Chandrakirti (Skt). The sixth century CE Indian Buddhist philosopher who wrote commentaries on Nagarjuna's philosophy. His best-known work is *A Guide to the Middle Way (Madhyamakavatara).* Tib:*u-ma-la juk-pä tsik-leur-jä pa).*

Cittamatra (Skt; Tib: sem tsam). Literally, the "mind-only" school of Mahayana philosophy. Roughly synonymous with Yogachara and Vijnanavada, Cittamatra defines the crucial concept of emptiness in terms of either an object's lack of difference from the subject perceiving it, or dependent phenomena's lack of the imaginary nature imputed to them. Tibetan tradition identifies two major types of Cittamatrins: those following scripture (e.g. Asanga) and those following reasoning (e.g. Dharmakirti). (See *The Crystal Mirror of Philosophical Systems*, p. 499.)

compassion (Skt: karuna; Tib: nying-je). The wish for all sentient beings to be separated from their mental and physical suffering. A prerequisite for the development of bodhicitta. Compassion is symbolized by the meditational deity Avalokiteshvara and the mantra OM MANI PADME HUM.

consciousness. See *mind*.

constituents, eighteen (Skt: dhatu; Tib: kham). The six sense powers, the six consciousnesses and the six objects.

cyclic existence. See *samsara*.

defilement. See *delusion*.

delusion (Skt: klesha; Tib: nyön-mong). An obscuration covering the essentially pure nature of mind, being thereby responsible for suffering and dissatisfaction; the main delusion is ignorance, out of which grow desirous attachment, hatred, jealousy and all the other delusions.

dependent origination (Skt: pratityasamutpada). Also called dependent arising. The way that the self and phenomena exist conventionally as relative and interdependent. They come into existence in dependence upon (1) causes and conditions, (2) their parts and, most subtly, (3) the mind imputing, or labeling, them. See also *twelve links*.

Dharma (Skt; Tib: chö). The second refuge jewel. Literally, "that which holds or protects (us from suffering)" and hence brings happiness and leads us towards liberation and enlightenment. In Buddhism, absolute Dharma is the realizations attained along the path to liberation and enlightenment and conventional Dharma is seen as both the teachings of the Buddha and virtuous actions.

dharmakaya (Skt; Tib: chö-ku; Eng: truth body). The truth body of a buddha (the other "body" being the form body or *rupakaya*); the blissful omniscient mind of a buddha, the result of the wisdom side of the path. It can be divided into the wisdom body (Skt: *jnanakaya*; Tib:*ye-she nyi-ku*) and the nature body (Skt: *svabhavikakaya*; Tib: *ngo-wo nyi-ku*). (See also *rupakaya* and *svabhavikakaya*).

dualistic view. The ignorant view characteristic of the unenlightened mind in which all things are falsely conceived to have concrete self-existence. To such a view, the appearance of an object is mixed with the false image of its being independent or self-existent, thereby leading to further dualistic views concerning subject and object, self and other, this and that and so forth.

emptiness (Skt: shunyata; Tib: tong-pa-nyi). Literally "emptiness *only.*" The absence, or lack, of true existence. Ultimately, every phenomenon is empty of existing truly, or from its own side, or independently. Lama Zopa Rinpoche explains the importance of the syllable *nyi* (Tib) or "only" in cutting off ordinary emptiness, for example, a purse being empty of having money. Without this final syllable the term falls short of indicating the total lack of inherent existence.

enlightenment (Skt: bodhi; Tib: jang-chub). Full awakening; buddhahood; omniscience. The ultimate goal of a Mahayana Buddhist, attained when all obscurations have been removed and all the qualities of the mind have been fully actualized. It is a state characterized by perfect compassion, wisdom and power. Lama Zopa Rinpoche points out that the Tibetan, *jang-chub,* is much more precise than the English as the two syllables encompass what enlightenment is: *jang* meaning "elimination" as in the elimination of all gross and subtle obstacles and *chub* meaning "development" as in the development of all perfect qualities.

five aggregates (Skt: skandha). The five psycho-physical constituents that make up a sentient being: form, feeling, discriminative awareness, conditioning (compositional) factors and consciousness.

five buddha lineages (Tib: rig-nga). Sometimes called the "five dhyani buddhas" or "five buddha types." The five buddhas that represent the five qualities of the Buddha. *Dhyana* is Sanskrit for "firm concentration." They are Vairochana, Akshobhya, Amitabha, Ratnasambhava and Amoghasiddhi.

five paths. The paths along which beings progress to liberation and enlightenment: the path of merit (Skt: *sambhara-marga;* Tib: *tsok-lam*), the path of preparation (Skt: *prayoga-marga;* Tib: *jor-lam*), the right-seeing path (Skt: *darsana-marga;* Tib: *tong-lam*), the path of meditation (Skt: *bhavana-marga;* Tib: *gom-lam*) and (the unification of) no more learning (Skt: *asaiksa-marga;* Tib: *mi-lop-pä-lam*).See *Liberation in Our Hands, Part 1,* p. 106, note 86.

form body. See *rupakaya.*

four noble truths. The subject of the Buddha's first turning of the wheel of Dharma. The truths of suffering, the origin of suffering, the cessation of suffering and the path to the cessation of suffering as seen by an *arya.*

graduated path of the three capable beings (Tib: kye-bu- sum gyi lam-gyi rim-pa). Also known as the three scopes or three levels of practice, the three levels of the lower, middle and higher capable being, based on the motivations of trying to attain a better future rebirth, liberation or enlightenment.

graduated path to enlightenment. See *lam-rim.*

Gelug (Tib). The Virtuous Order. The order of Tibetan Buddhism founded by Lama Tsongkhapa and his disciples in the early fifteenth century and the most recent of the four main schools of Tibetan Buddhism. Developed from the Kadam school founded by Atisha and Dromtönpa. Cf. *Nyingma, Kagyü* and *Sakya.*

Great Vehicle. See *Mahayana.*

Hearer Vehicle. See *Shravakayana.*

Heaven of Thirty-three (Skt: Trayastrimsha; Tib: Sum-chu tsa-sum). The highest of the god realm abodes in Buddhist cosmology; it is atop Mount Meru and ruled by Indra.

Hinayana (Skt). Literally, Small, or Lesser, Vehicle. It is one of the two general divisions of Buddhism. Hinayana practitioners' motivation for following the Dharma path is principally their intense wish for personal liberation from samsara. Two types of Hinayana practitioner are identified: hearers and solitary realizers. Cf. *Mahayana.*

ignorance (Skt: avidya; Tib: ma-rig-pa). Literally, "not seeing" that which exists, or the way in which things exist. There are basically two kinds, ignorance of karma and ignorance of ultimate truth. The fundamental delusion from which all others spring. The first of the twelve links of dependent origination.

impermanence (Tib: mi-tag-pa). The gross and subtle levels of the transience of phenomena. The moment things and events come into existence, their disintegration has already begun.

inherent (or intrinsic) existence. What phenomena are empty of; the object of negation, or refutation. To ignorance, phenomena appear to exist independently, in and of themselves; to exist inherently. Cf. *emptiness*.

intermediate state (Tib: bar-do). The state between death and rebirth. For details, see Lati Rinbochay & Jeffrey Hopkins. *Death, Intermediate State and Rebirth*. Ithaca: Snow Lion Publications, 1980.

Jataka Tales. Stories of the lives of the historical Buddha before he became enlightened.

Kadam (Tib). The order of Tibetan Buddhism founded in the eleventh century by Atisha, Dromtönpa and their followers, the "Kadampa geshes"; the forerunner of the Gelug school, whose members are sometimes called the New Kadampas.

Kagyü (Tib). The order of Tibetan Buddhism founded in the eleventh century by Marpa, Milarepa, Gampopa and their followers. One of the four main schools of Tibetan Buddhism. Cf. *Nyingma*, *Sakya* and *Gelug*.

Kangyur (Tib). The part of the Tibetan Canon that contains the sutras and tantras; literally, "translation of the (Buddha's) word." It contains 108 volumes.

karma (Skt; Tib: lä). Action; the working of cause and effect, whereby positive (virtuous) actions produce happiness and negative (nonvirtuous) actions produce suffering.

kaya (Skt). Buddha-, or holy, body. A body of an enlightened being. See also *dharmakaya* and *rupakaya*.

klesha (Skt). See *delusion*.

lama (Tib; Skt: guru). A spiritual guide or teacher. One who shows a disciple the path to liberation and enlightenment. Literally, heavy—heavy with knowledge of Dharma.

lam-rim (Tib). The graduated path. A presentation of Shakyamuni Buddha's teachings in a form suitable for the step-by-step training of a disciple. See also *Atisha* and *three principal aspects of the path*.

Lesser Vehicle. See *Hinayana*.

liberation (Skt: nirvana, or moksha; Tib: myang-dä, or thar-pa).The state of complete freedom from samsara; the goal of a practitioner seeking his or her own escape from suffering (see also *Hinayana*). "Lower nirvana" is used to refer to this state of self-liberation, while "higher nirvana" refers to the supreme attainment of the full enlightenment of buddhahood. Natural nirvana (*Tib: rang-zhin myang-dä*) is the fundamentally pure nature of reality, where all things and events are devoid of any inherent, intrinsic or independent reality.

Madhyamaka (Skt; Tib: u-ma). The Middle Way school of Buddhist philosophy; a system of analysis founded by Nagarjuna based on the *prajnaparamita* sutras of Shakyamuni Buddha and considered to be the supreme presentation of the wisdom of emptiness. This view holds that all phenomena are dependent originations and thereby avoids the mistaken extremes of self-existence and non-existence, or eternalism and nihilism. It has two divisions, *Svatantrika* and *Prasangika*. With *Cittamatra*, it is one of the two Mahayana schools of philosophy, and with the two Hinayana schools, the *Vaibhashika* and *Sautrantika*, one of the four main schools of Buddhist philosophy.

Mahayana (Skt). Literally, Great Vehicle. It is one of the two general divisions of Buddhism. Mahayana practitioners' motivation for following the Dharma path is principally their intense wish for all mother sentient beings to be liberated from conditioned existence, or samsara, and to attain the full enlightenment of buddhahood. The Mahayana has two divisions, *Paramitayana* (Sutrayana) and *Vajrayana* (Tantrayana, Mantrayana). Cf. *Hinayana*.

Maitreya (Skt; Tib: Jam-pa). After Shakyamuni Buddha, the next (fifth) of the thousand buddhas of this fortunate eon to descend to turn the wheel of Dharma. Presently residing in the pure land of Tushita

(Ganden). Recipient of the method lineage of Shakyamuni Buddha's teachings, which, in a mystical transmission, he passed on to Asanga.

Manjushri (Skt; Tib: Jam-päl-yang). The bodhisattva (or buddha) of wisdom. Recipient of the wisdom lineage of Shakyamuni Buddha's teachings, which he passed on to Nagarjuna.

mantra (Skt Tib: ngag). Literally, mind protection. Mantras are Sanskrit syllables—usually recited in conjunction with the practice of a particular meditational deity—and embody the qualities of the deity with which they are associated.

mara (Skt). See *obstructive forces.*

Marpa (1012–96). Founder of the Kagyü tradition of Tibetan Buddhism, he was a renowned tantric master and translator, a disciple of Naropa and the guru of Milarepa.

meditation (Tib: gom). Familiarization of the mind with a virtuous object. There are two types, placement (absorptive) and analytic (insight).

merit. Positive imprints left on the mind by virtuous, or Dharma, actions. The principal cause of happiness. Accumulation of merit, when coupled with the accumulation of wisdom, eventually results in rupakaya.

Middle Way school. See *Madhyamaka.*

Milarepa (1040–1123). Tibet's great yogi, who achieved enlightenment in his lifetime under the tutelage of his guru, Marpa, who was a contemporary of Atisha. One of the founding fathers of the Kagyü school.

mind (Skt: citta; Tib: sem). Synonymous with consciousness (*Skt: vijnana; Tib: nam-she*) and sentience (*Skt: manas; Tib: yi*). Defined as that which is "clear and knowing"; a formless entity that has the ability to perceive objects. Mind is divided into six primary consciousnesses and fifty-one mental factors.

Mind Only school. See *Cittamatra.*

Nagarjuna. The great second-century Indian philosopher and tantric adept who propounded the Madhyamaka philosophy of emptiness. He is one of six great Indian scholars, known as the Six Ornaments. See *Meditation on Emptiness,* pp. 356-359.

Naropa (1016–1100). The Indian mahasiddha, a disciple of Tilopa and guru of Marpa and Maitripa, who transmitted many tantric lineages, including that of the renowned *Six Yogas of Naropa*.

nihilism. The doctrine that nothing exists; that, for example, there's no cause and effect of actions or no past and future lives.

nirmanakaya (Skt; Tib: trul-ku; Eng: emanation body). The emanation body of a buddha that manifests in a variety of forms for sentient beings See also *rupakaya*.

nirvana (Skt). See *liberation*.

Nyingma (Tib). The old translation school of Tibetan Buddhism, which traces its teachings back to the time of Padmasambhava, the eighth century Indian tantric master invited to Tibet by King Trisong Detsen to clear away hindrances to the establishment of Buddhism in Tibet. The first of the four main schools of Tibetan Buddhism. Cf. *Kagyü, Sakya* and *Gelug*.

object of negation, or refutation (Tib: gag-cha). What is conceived by an awareness conceiving true existence; the appearance of inherent existence.

obscurations, obstructions (Skt: avarana; Tib: drib). Also known as obstructions; the negative imprints left on the mind by negative karma and delusion, which obscure the mind. The disturbing-thought obscurations (Tib: *nyön-drib*) obstruct attainment of liberation and the more subtle obscurations to knowledge (Tib: *she-drib*) obstruct the attainment of enlightenment.

obstructive forces (Skt: mara), four. The afflictions, death, the five aggregates and the "divine youth demon."

paramita (Skt). See *six perfections*.

Paramitayana (Skt). The Perfection Vehicle; the first of the two Mahayana paths. This is the gradual path to enlightenment traversed by bodhisattvas practicing the six perfections through the ten bodhisattva levels (*bhumi*) over countless eons of rebirth in samsara for the benefit of all sentient beings. Also called Sutrayana or Bodhisattvayana. Cf. *Vajrayana*.

path(s) of merit, preparation, right-seeing. See *five paths*.

penetrative insight. See *vipashyana.*

Perfection Vehicle. See *Paramitayana.*

pervasive compounding suffering. The third and most subtle of the three
types of suffering explained by the Buddha referring to the nature of
the five aggregates, which are contaminated by karma and delusions.
See also *suffering of suffering* and *suffering of change.*

Prajnaparamita (Skt). The *Perfection of Wisdom.* The *Prajnaparamita
Sutras* are the teachings of Shakyamuni Buddha in which the wisdom
of emptiness and the path of the bodhisattva are set forth. The basis of
Nagarjuna's philosophy.

*Prasangika Madhyamaka (Skt; Tib: u ma thäl gyur).*The Middle Way Consequence School, a sub-school of the Middle Way school of Buddhist
philosophy. According to Tibetan scholarly tradition, the school of
Madhyamaka philosophy that (a) stresses the use of *reductio ad absurdum (prasanga)* rather than syllogistic reasoning in establishing emptiness as the nature of dharmas and (b) denies that dharmas possess
inherent defining characteristics *(svalaksana)* even conventionally. The
greatest Indian representative of the Prasangika is generally regarded
to be Chandrakirti. (See *The Crystal Mirror of Philosophical Systems,*
p. 508.) See also *Madhyamaka* and *Svatantrika Madhyamaka.*

Pratimoksha (Skt). The various levels of individual liberation vows for lay
and ordained, including the five lay vows (Tib: *ge-nyen*) and the novice
vows and full ordination that monks and nuns take.

Pratyekabuddhayana (Skt). The Solitary Realizer Vehicle. One of the
branches of the Hinayana. Practitioners who strive for nirvana in sol-
itude, without relying on a teacher. Cf. *Sharavakayana.*

preta (Skt). Hungry ghost, or spirit. The preta realm is one of the three
lower realms of cyclic existence. See *Liberation in Our Hands, Part 2,*
p. 161 ff. for a detailed discussion.

purification. The eradication from the mind of negative imprints left by
past nonvirtuous actions, which would otherwise ripen into suffering.
The most effective methods of purification employ the four opponent
powers of regret, reliance, virtuous activity and resolve.

puja (Skt). Literally, offering; usually used to describe an offering ceremony such as the *Offering to the Spiritual Master* (*Guru Puja*).

refuge (Skt: sharana; Tib: kyab). The door to the Dharma path. Having taken refuge from the heart we become an inner being or Buddhist. There are three levels of refuge—Hinayana, Mahayana and Vajrayana—and two or three causes necessary for taking refuge: fearing the sufferings of samsara in general and lower realms in particular; faith that Buddha, Dharma and Sangha have the qualities and power to lead us to happiness, liberation and enlightenment; and (for Mahayana refuge) compassion for all sentient beings.

renunciation (Tib: nge-jung). Literally "definite emergence." The state of mind not having the slightest attraction to samsaric pleasures for even a second and having the strong wish for liberation. The first of the three principal aspects of the path to enlightenment. Cf. *bodhicitta* and *right view*.

right view. See *emptiness*.

rinpoche (Tib). Literally, "precious one." Epithet for an incarnate lama, that is one who has intentionally taken rebirth in a human form to benefit sentient beings on the path to enlightenment.

rupakaya (Skt; Tib: zug-ku; Eng: form body). The form body of a fully enlightened being; the result of the complete and perfect accumulation of merit. It has two aspects: *sambhogakaya*, (enjoyment body), in which the enlightened mind appears to benefit highly realized bodhisattvas, and *nirmanakaya*, (emanation body), in which the enlightened mind appears to benefit ordinary beings. See also *dharmakaya*.

Sakya (Tib). One of the four main schools of Tibetan Buddhism. It was founded in the south of the province of Tsang by Khön Könchog Gyälpo (1034–1102). Cf. *Nyingma*, *Kagyü* and *Gelug*.

samadhi. See *single-pointed concentration*.

sambhogakaya (Skt; Tib: long-ku; Eng: enjoyment body) The enjoyment body; the form in which the enlightened mind appears in order to benefit highly realized bodhisattvas. See also *rupakaya*.

samsara (Skt; Tib: khor-wa). The six realms of conditioned existence, three lower—hell, hungry ghost (*Skt: preta*) and animal—and three upper—

human, demigod (*Skt: asura*) and god (*Skt: sura*); the beginningless, recurring cycle of death and rebirth under the control of delusion and karma and fraught with suffering. It also refers to the contaminated aggregates of a sentient being.

Sangha (Skt; Tib: ge-dün). Spiritual community; the third of the Three Rare Sublime Ones or Three Jewels of Refuge. In Tibetan *ge-dün* literally means intending (*dün*) to virtue (*ge*). Absolute Sangha are those who have directly realized emptiness; relative Sangha refers to a group of at least four fully ordained monks or nuns.

Sautrantika (Skt; Tib: do-de-pa). According to Tibetan traditions, one of the two major Hinayana philosophical schools. Ontologically, Sautrantikas subscribe to a doctrine of radical momentariness and accept some dharmas as real and others as conceptual; epistemologically, they assert a representational realism. Vasubandhu's *Autocommentary on the Treasury of Higher Knowledge* reflects Sautrantika views, as do some of the writings of Dignaga and Dharmakirti. (See *The Crystal Mirror of Philosophical Systems*, p. 508.)

sentient being (Tib: sem-chen). Any unenlightened being; any being whose mind is not completely free from gross and subtle ignorance.

Shakyamuni Buddha (563-483 BC). Fourth of the one thousand founding buddhas of this present world age. Born a prince of the Shakya clan in north India, he taught the sutra and tantra paths to liberation and enlightenment; founder of what came to be known as Buddhism. (From the *Skt: buddha*—"fully awake.")

shamatha (Skt; Tib: shi-nä). Calm abiding; stabilization arisen from meditation and conjoined with special pliancy. See, for example, *Meditation on Emptiness*, pp. 67-90.

Shravakayana (Skt). The Hearer Vehicle. One of the branches of the Hinayana. Practitioners (hearers, or *shravakas*) who strive for nirvana on the basis of listening to teachings from a teacher. Cf. *Pratyekabuddhayana.*

shunyata. See *emptiness.*

single-pointed concentration (Skt: samadhi; Tib: ting-nge-dzin). A state of deep meditative absorption; single-pointed concentration on the actual nature of things, free from discursive thought and dualistic conceptions.

six perfections (Skt: paramita). Generosity, morality, patience, enthusiastic perseverance, concentration and wisdom. See also *Paramitayana*.

skandha (Skt). The five psychophysical constituents that make up a sentient being: form, feeling, discriminative awareness, conditioning (compositional) factors and consciousness.

Solitary Realizer Vehicle. See *Pratyekabuddhayana*.

sources, twelve (Skt: ayatana; Tib: kye-che). The six internal sources (of consciousness) are the eye, ear, nose, tongue, body and mental sense powers; the six external sources (of consciousness or fields of consciousness) are the form source, sound source, odor source, taste source, object-of-touch source and phenomenon source.

suffering of change. The second of the three types of suffering explained by the Buddha, how temporary samsaric pleasures are by nature unsatisfactory and therefore suffering. See also *suffering of suffering* and *pervasive compounding suffering*.

suffering of suffering. The first of the three types of suffering explained by the Buddha, the easily discernible mental and physical pain and discomfort we all try to avoid. See also *suffering of change* and *pervasive compounding suffering*.

sutra (Skt). A discourse of Shakyamuni Buddha; the pre-tantric division of Buddhist teachings stressing the cultivation of bodhicitta and the practice of the six perfections. See also *Paramitayana*.

Sutrayana (Skt). The Sutra Vehicle, another name for *Bodhisattvayana* or *Paramitayana*; the non-tantric path that encompasses both Hinayana practices such as the *thirty-seven wings of enlightenment* and Mahayana bodhisattva practices such as the *six perfections*, in order to gather the two accumulations of merit and wisdom, the respective causes of the rupakaya and the dharmakaya, hence its other name, the causal vehicle.

svabhavikakaya (Skt; Tib: ngo-wo nyi-ku; Eng: nature body). The essential purity of the mind that is the *dharmakaya* (truth body). See *Liberation in Our Hands, Part 2*, p. 289.

Svatantrika Madhyamaka (Skt; Tib: u ma rang gyü). The Middle Way Autonomy School, a sub-school of the Middle Way school of Buddhist philosophy. According to Tibetan scholarly tradition, the school of Madhyamaka philosophy that (a) stresses syllogistic reasoning rather than the use of *reductio ad absurdum (prasanga)* in establishing the nature of dharmas as emptiness and (b) asserts that dharmas possess inherent defining characteristics *(svalaksana)*, at least conventionally. The school is subdivided into Sautrantika Svatantrika Madhyamaka (represented by Bhavaviveka and Jnanagarbha) and Yogachara Svatantrika Madhyamaka (represented by Santarakshita and Kamalasila). (See *The Crystal Mirror of Philosophical Systems,* p. 510.) See also *Madhyamaka* and *Prasangika Madhyamaka.*

tantra (Skt; Tib: gyü). Literally, thread, or continuity; the texts of the secret mantra teachings of Buddhism. Often used to refer to these teachings themselves. See also *Vajrayana.* Cf. *sutra.*

Tantrayana (Skt). See *Vajrayana.*

Tengyur (Tib). The part of the Tibetan Canon that contains the Indian pandits' commentaries on the Buddha's teachings. Literally, "translation of the commentaries." It contains about 225 volumes (depending on the edition).

ten nonvirtuous actions. Three of body (killing, stealing, sexual misconduct); four of speech (lying, speaking harshly, slandering and gossiping); and three of mind (covetousness, ill will and wrong views). General actions to be avoided so as not to create negative karma.

Theravada (Skt). A tradition of Buddhism that upholds the Pali Canon and the noble eightfold path, which leads practitioners to liberation(nirvana), a state free from the suffering of conditioned existence; one of the eighteen schools into which the Hinayana split not long after Shakyamuni Buddha's death; the dominant Hinayana school today, widely practiced in Sri Lanka and most of continental South-east Asia.

three baskets. See *tripitaka.*

Three Higher Trainings. Morality (ethics), meditation (concentration) and wisdom (insight).

Three Jewels (Skt: triratna; Tib: kön-chog-sum). Also called the Triple Gem or the Three Rare Sublime Ones. The objects of Buddhist refuge: Buddha, Dharma and Sangha. Lama Zopa Rinpoche prefers "Three Rare Sublime Ones" as a more direct translation of *kön-chog-sum.*

three principal aspects of the path. The three main divisions of the lam-rim: renunciation, bodhicitta and the right view (of emptiness).

three scopes. See *graduated path of the three capable beings.*

tripitaka (Skt). The three divisions of the Dharma into vinaya, sutra and abhidharma.

Triple Gem. See *Three Jewels.*

tsampa. Roasted barley flour; a Tibetan staple food.

Tsongkhapa, Lama Je (1357-1417). Founder of the Gelug tradition of Tibetan Buddhism and revitalizer of many sutra and tantra lineages and the monastic tradition in Tibet.

twelve links of dependent origination. (Skt: pratitya samutpada; Tib: ten-drel chu-nyi). Also called the twelve dependent-related limbs or branches; the twelve steps in the evolution of cyclic existence: ignorance, karmic formation, consciousness, name and form, sensory fields, contact, feelings, attachment, grasping, becoming (existence), birth and aging and death. This is Shakyamuni Buddha's explanation of how delusion and karma bind sentient beings to samsara, causing them to be reborn into suffering again and again; depicted pictorially in the Tibetan *Wheel of Life.*

Vaibhashika (Skt; Tib: je-dra ma-wa). The Great Exposition (Hinayana) school of the four schools of Buddhist philosophy.

Vajrayana (Skt). The adamantine vehicle; the second of the two Mahayana paths; also called Tantrayana or Mantrayana. This is the quickest vehicle of Buddhism as it allows certain practitioners to attain enlightenment within a single lifetime. See also *tantra.*

vinaya (Skt; Tib: dül-wa). The Buddha's teachings on ethical discipline (morality), monastic conduct and so forth; one of the three baskets.

vipashyana (Skt; Tib: lhag-tong). Penetrative (special) insight; a wisdom of thorough discrimination of phenomenon conjoined with special pliancy induced by the power of analysis. Cf. insight meditation (Pali: *vipassana*), the principal meditation taught in the Hinayana tradition, based on the Buddha's teachings on the four foundations of mindfulness. See, for example, *Meditation on Emptiness*, pp. 91-109.

vows of individual liberation. See *pratimoksha.*

wisdom. Different levels of insight into the nature of reality. There are, for example, the three wisdoms of hearing, contemplation and meditation. Ultimately, there is the wisdom realizing emptiness, which frees beings from cyclic existence and eventually brings them to enlightenment. The complete and perfect accumulation of wisdom results in dharmakaya. Cf. *merit.*

BIBLIOGRAPHY

Aryadeva and Gyel-tsap. *Yogic Deeds of Bodhisattvas: Gyel-tsap on Aryadeva's Four Hundred.* Commentary by Geshe Sonam Rinchen, translated and edited by Ruth Sonam. Ithaca: Snow Lion Publications, 1994.

Atisha Dipamkara Shrijnana. *Atisha's Lamp for the Path to Enlightenment.* Commentary by Geshe Sonam Rinchen, translated and edited by Ruth Sonam. Ithaca: Snow Lion Publications, 1997.

——. *The Complete Works of Atisha: The Lamp for the Path, the Commentary, together with the newly translated Twenty-five Key Texts.* Translated and annotated by Richard Sherburne, SJ. New Delhi: Aditya Prakashan, 2009.

Chandrakirti. *Guide to the Middle Way. Madhyamakavatara.* Chapters 1–5) in Jeffrey Hopkins, *Compassion in Tibetan Buddhism*, Ithaca: Snow Lion Publications, 1985. Chapter 6 in Geshe Rabten, *Echoes of Voidness*, Stephen Batchelor (trans.), Boston: Wisdom Publications, 1983. Complete English translation by C. W. Huntington, Jr. and Geshe Namgyal Wangchen in *The Emptiness of Emptiness: An Introduction to Early Indian Madhyamika.* Hawaii: University of Hawaii Press, 1989.

Cozort, Daniel, and Craig Preston. *Buddhist Philosophy: Losang Gönchok's Short Commentary to Jamyang Shayba's Root Text on Tenets.* Ithaca: Snow Lion Publications, 2003.

The Dalai Lama. *Healing Anger: The Power of Patience from a Buddhist Perspective.* Translated by Geshe Thupten Jinpa. Ithaca: Snow Lion Publications, 1997.

——. *Illuminating the Path to Enlightenment: A Commentary on Atisha Dipamkara Shrijnana's A Lamp for the Path to Enlightenment and Lama Je Tsong Khapa's Lines of Experience.* Translated by Geshe Thupten Jinpa. Edited by Rebecca McClen Novick, Thupten Jinpa and Nicholas Ribush. Long Beach: Gaden Shartse Thubten Dhargye Ling, 2002.

——. *The Meaning of Life: Buddhist Perspectives on Cause and Effect*. Translated and edited by Jeffrey Hopkins. Boston: Wisdom Publications, 2000.

——. *Opening the Eye of New Awareness*. Translated and introduced by Donald S. Lopez, Jr. Boston: Wisdom Publications, 1999.

——. *Practicing Wisdom: The Perfection of Shantideva's Bodhisattva Way*. Translated and edited by Thupten Jinpa. Boston: Wisdom Publications, 2005.

——. *The World of Tibetan Buddhism: An Overview of Its Philosophy and Practice*. Translated, edited and annotated by Geshe Thupten Jinpa. Boston: Wisdom Publications, 1995.

FPMT. *Essential Buddhist Prayers: An FPMT Prayer Book, Volume 1: Basic Prayers and Practices*. Various authors. Portland: FPMT Publications, 2011.

Hellbach, Michael (ed.). *From Tushita*. Dharamsala and Duisburg: Tushita Publications, 1977.

Hopkins, Jeffrey. *Meditation on Emptiness*. Boston: Wisdom Publications, 1983, 1996.

Komito, David Ross. *Nagarjuna's "Seventy Stanzas": A Buddhist Psychology of Emptiness*. Ithaca: Snow Lion Publications, 1987.

Lati Rinbochay and Denma Lochö Rinbochay. *Meditative States in Tibetan Buddhism*. Translated by Leah Zahler and Jeffrey Hopkins. Boston: Wisdom Publications, 1997.

Mullin, Glenn H., and Nicholas Ribush (eds.). *Teachings at Tushita: An Anthology of Buddhist Teachings*. New Delhi: Mahayana Publications, 1981.

Nagarjuna. *Buddhist Advice for Living and Liberation: Nagarjuna's Precious Garland*. Analyzed, translated and edited by Jeffrey Hopkins. Ithaca: Snow Lion Publications, 1998.

——. *The Fundamental Wisdom of the Middle Way: Nagarjuna's Mulamadhyamakakarika*. Translation and commentary by Jay L. Garfield. New York: Oxford University Press, 1995.

Pabongka Rinpoche. *Liberation in Our Hands, Parts 1, 2 and 3*. Transcribed and edited by Yongzin Trijang Rinpoche Losang Yeshe Tenzin Gyatso. Translated by Geshe Lobsang Tharchin with Artemus B. Engle. Howell: Mahayana Sutra and Tantra Press, 1990, 1994, 2001.

——. *Liberation in the Palm of your Hand: A Concise Discourse on the Path to Enlightenment*. Edited by Trijang Rinpoche. Translated by Michael Richards. Boston: Wisdom Publications, 2006.

Rabten, Geshe, and Geshe Dhargyey. *Advice from a Spiritual Friend*. Boston: Wisdom Publications, 1977 and 1996.

Shantideva. *A Guide to the Bodhisattva's Way of Life*. Translated by Stephen Batchelor. Dharamsala: Library of Tibetan Works and Archives, 1979, 2007.

———. *Shiksa-Samuccaya: A Compendium of Buddhist Doctrine*. Translated by Cecil Bendall & WHD Rouse. Delhi: Motilal Banarsidass, 1971.

Sopa, Geshe Lhundup, and Jeffrey Hopkins. *Cutting Through Appearances: Practice and Theory of Tibetan Buddhism*. Ithaca: Snow Lion Publications, 1989.

Tsong-kha-pa (as Tsong Khapa Losang Drakpa). *Great Treatise on the Stages of Mantra (sngags rim chen mo): Critical Elucidation of the Key Instructions in All the Secret Stages of the Path of the Victorious Universal Lord, Great Vajradhara. Chapters XI–XII. The Creation Stage*. Introduced and translated by Thomas Freeman Yarnall. New York: American Institute of Buddhist Studies, 2013.

———. *The Great Treatise on the Stages of the Path to Enlightenment (Lamrim Chenmo): Volumes One to Three*. Lamrim Chenmo Translation Committee. Editor-in-Chief, Joshua W. C. Cutler; editor, Guy Newland. Ithaca: Snow Lion Publications, 2000, 2002 and 2004.

Zopa Rinpoche, Lama *The Heart of the Path: Seeing the Guru as Buddha*. Edited by Ailsa Cameron. Boston: Lama Yeshe Wisdom Archive, 2009.

LAMA YESHE WISDOM ARCHIVE

The LAMA YESHE WISDOM ARCHIVE (LYWA) is the collected works of Lama Thubten Yeshe and Lama Thubten Zopa Rinpoche. Lama Zopa Rinpoche, its spiritual director, founded the ARCHIVE in 1996. Lama Yeshe and Lama Zopa Rinpoche began teaching at Kopan Monastery, Nepal, in 1970. Since then, their teachings have been recorded and transcribed. At present we have well over 12,000 hours of digital audio and some 90,000 pages of raw transcript. Many recordings, mostly teachings by Lama Zopa Rinpoche, remain to be transcribed, and as Rinpoche continues to teach, the number of recordings in the ARCHIVE increases accordingly. Most of our transcripts have been neither checked nor edited.

Here at the LYWA we are making every effort to organize the transcription of that which has not yet been transcribed, edit that which has not yet been edited, and generally do the many other tasks detailed below.

The work of the LAMA YESHE WISDOM ARCHIVE falls into two categories: *archiving* and *dissemination*.

Archiving requires managing the recordings of teachings by Lama Yeshe and Lama Zopa Rinpoche that have already been collected, collecting recordings of teachings given but not yet sent to the ARCHIVE, and collecting recordings of Lama Zopa's on-going teachings, talks, advice and so forth as he travels the world for the benefit of all. Incoming media are then catalogued and stored safely while being kept accessible for further work.

We organize the transcription of audio, add the transcripts to the already existent database of teachings, manage this database, have transcripts checked, and make transcripts available to editors or others doing research on or practicing these teachings.

Other archiving activities include working with video and photographs of the Lamas and digitizing ARCHIVE materials.

Dissemination involves keeping up with evolving technology and making the Lamas' teachings available through various avenues including books for free distribution and sale, ebooks on a wide range of readers, lightly edited transcripts, a monthly e-letter (see below), social media, DVDs and online video, articles in Mandala and other magazines and on our website. Irrespective of the medium we choose, the teachings require a significant amount of work to prepare them for distribution.

This is just a summary of what we do. The ARCHIVE was established with virtually no seed funding and has developed solely through the kindness of many people, most of whom we mention and thank sincerely on our website. We are indebted to you all.

Our further development similarly depends upon the generosity of those who see the benefit and necessity of this work, and we would be extremely grateful for your help. Thus we hereby appeal to you for your kind support. If you would like to make a contribution to help us with any of the above tasks or to sponsor books for free distribution, please contact us:

LAMA YESHE WISDOM ARCHIVE
PO Box 636, Lincoln, MA 01773, USA
Telephone (781) 259-4466
info@LamaYeshe.com
LamaYeshe.com

The LAMA YESHE WISDOM ARCHIVE is a 501(c)(3) tax-deductible, non-profit corporation dedicated to the welfare of all sentient beings and totally dependent upon your donations for its continued existence. Thank you so much for your support. You may contribute by mailing a check, bank draft or money order to our Lincoln address; by making a donation on our secure website; by mailing us your credit card number or phoning it in; or by transferring funds directly to our bank—ask us for details.

LAMA YESHE WISDOM ARCHIVE MEMBERSHIP

In order to raise the money we need to employ editors to make available the thousands of hours of teachings mentioned above, we have established a membership plan. Membership costs US$1,000 and its main benefit is that you will be helping make the Lamas' incredible teachings available to a worldwide audience. More direct and tangible benefits to you personally include free Lama Yeshe and Lama Zopa Rinpoche books from the ARCHIVE and Wisdom Publications, a year's subscription to *Mandala*, a year of monthly pujas by the monks and nuns at Kopan Monastery with your personal dedication, and access to an exclusive members-only section of our website containing the entire LYWA library of publications in electronic format. Please see www.LamaYeshe.com for more information.

MONTHLY E-LETTER

Each month we send out a free e-letter containing our latest news and a previously unpublished teaching by Lama Yeshe or Lama Zopa Rinpoche. To see over 140 back-issues or to subscribe with your email address, please go to our website.

The Foundation for the Preservation of the Mahayana Tradition

The Foundation for the Preservation of the Mahayana Tradition (FPMT) is an international organization of Buddhist meditation study and retreat centers—both urban and rural—monasteries, publishing houses, healing centers and other related activities founded in 1975 by Lama Thubten Yeshe and Lama Thubten Zopa Rinpoche. At present, there are more than 160 FPMT centers, projects and services in over forty countries worldwide.

The FPMT has been established to facilitate the study and practice of Mahayana Buddhism in general and the Tibetan Gelug tradition, founded in the fifteenth century by the great scholar, yogi and saint, Lama Je Tsongkhapa, in particular.

Every quarter, the Foundation publishes a wonderful news journal, *Mandala*, from its International Office in the United States of America. To subscribe or view back-issues, please go to the *Mandala* website, www. mandalamagazine.org, or contact:

FPMT
1632 SE 11th Avenue, Portland, OR 97214
Telephone (503) 808-1588; Fax (503) 808-1589
info@fpmt.org
www.fpmt.org

The FPMT website also offers teachings by His Holiness the Dalai Lama, Lama Yeshe, Lama Zopa Rinpoche and many other highly respected teachers in the tradition, details about the FPMT's educational programs, an online learning center, a complete listing of FPMT centers all over the world and, especially, those in your area, a link to the excellent FPMT Store, and links to FPMT centers—where you will find details of their programs—and other interesting Buddhist and Tibetan pages.

FPMT Online Learning Center

In 2009, FPMT Education Services launched the FPMT Online Learning Center to make FPMT education programs and materials more accessible to students worldwide. While continuing to expand, the Online Learning Center currently offers the following courses:

- Meditation 101
- Buddhism in a Nutshell
- Heart Advice for Death and Dying
- Discovering Buddhism
- Basic Program
- Living in the Path
- Special Commentaries

Living in the Path is particularly unique in that it takes teachings by Lama Zopa Rinpoche and presents them in theme-related modules that include teaching transcripts, video extracts, meditations, mindfulness practices, karma yoga, and questions to assist students in integrating the material. Current modules include: *Motivation for Life, Taking the Essence, What Buddhists Believe, Guru is Buddha, Introduction to Atisha's text, The Happiness of Dharma, Bringing Emptiness to Life, The Secret of the Mind, Diamond Cutter Meditation, Refuge & Bodhicitta* and *Seven-Limb Prayer*.

All of our online programs provide audio and/or video teachings of the subjects, guided meditations, readings, and other support materials. Online forums for each program provide students the opportunity to discuss the subject matter and to ask questions of forum elders. Additionally, many retreats led by Lama Zopa Rinpoche are available in full via audio and/or video format.

Education Services is committed to creating a dynamic virtual learning environment and adding more FPMT programming and materials for you to enjoy via the Online Learning Center.

Visit us at: onlinelearning.fpmt.org

OTHER TEACHINGS OF LAMA YESHE AND LAMA ZOPA RINPOCHE CURRENTLY AVAILABLE

BOOKS PUBLISHED BY WISDOM PUBLICATIONS
Wisdom Energy, by Lama Yeshe and Lama Zopa Rinpoche
Introduction to Tantra, by Lama Yeshe
Transforming Problems, by Lama Zopa Rinpoche
The Door to Satisfaction, by Lama Zopa Rinpoche
Becoming Vajrasattva: The Tantric Path of Purification, by Lama Yeshe
The Bliss of Inner Fire, by Lama Yeshe
Becoming the Compassion Buddha, by Lama Yeshe
Ultimate Healing, by Lama Zopa Rinpoche
Dear Lama Zopa, by Lama Zopa Rinpoche
How to Be Happy, by Lama Zopa Rinpoche
Wholesome Fear, by Lama Zopa Rinpoche with Kathleen McDonald
When the Chocolate Runs Out, by Lama Yeshe

About Lama Yeshe: *Reincarnation: The Boy Lama*, by Vicki Mackenzie

About Lama Zopa Rinpoche: *The Lawudo Lama*, by Jamyang Wangmo

You can get more information about and order the above titles at wisdompubs.
org or call toll free in the USA on 1-800-272-4050.

TRANSCRIPTS, PRACTICES AND OTHER MATERIALS
See the LYWA and FPMT websites for transcripts of teachings by Lama Yeshe
and Lama Zopa Rinpoche and other practices written or compiled by Lama
Zopa Rinpoche.

VIDEO OF LAMA YESHE AND LAMA ZOPA RINPOCHE
LYWA has released DVDs of early teachings of the Lamas, including *The Three
Principal Aspects of the Path*, *Introduction to Tantra*, *Offering Tsok to Heruka
Vajrasattva*, *Anxiety in the Nuclear Age*, *Bringing Dharma to the West*, *Lama
Yeshe at Disneyland*, *Freedom Through Understanding* and *Life, Death and
After Death*. See LamaYeshe.com to order any of these DVDs or visit our You-
Tube channel to view these and many other videos for free: YouTube.com/
LamaYeshe.

FPMT has produced a number of DVDs of Lama Zopa Rinpoche's more recent
teachings. Visit the FPMT Foundation Store to order. Many more videos are
freely available at FPMT.org, and on FPMT's YouTube channel, YouTube.com/
FPMTInc.

What to do with Dharma teachings

The Buddhadharma is the true source of happiness for all sentient beings. Books like this show you how to put the teachings into practice and integrate them into your life, whereby you get the happiness you seek. Therefore, anything containing Dharma teachings, the names of your teachers or holy images is more precious than other material objects and should be treated with respect. To avoid creating the karma of not meeting the Dharma again in future lives, please do not put books (or other holy objects) on the floor or underneath other stuff, step over or sit upon them, or use them for mundane purposes such as propping up wobbly chairs or tables. They should be kept in a clean, high place, separate from worldly writings, and wrapped in cloth when being carried around. These are but a few considerations.

Should you need to get rid of Dharma materials, they should not be thrown in the rubbish but burned in a special way. Briefly: do not incinerate such materials with other trash, but alone, and as they burn, recite the mantra OM AH HUM. As the smoke rises, visualize that it pervades all of space, carrying the essence of the Dharma to all sentient beings in the six samsaric realms, purifying their minds, alleviating their suffering, and bringing them all happiness, up to and including enlightenment. Some people might find this practice a bit unusual, but it is given according to tradition. Thank you very much.

Dedication
Through the merit created by preparing, reading, thinking about and sharing this book with others, may all teachers of the Dharma live long and healthy lives, may the Dharma spread throughout the infinite reaches of space, and may all sentient beings quickly attain enlightenment.

In whichever realm, country, area or place this book may be, may there be no war, drought, famine, disease, injury, disharmony or unhappiness, may there be only great prosperity, may everything needed be easily obtained, and may all be guided by only perfectly qualified Dharma teachers, enjoy the happiness of Dharma, have love and compassion for all sentient beings, and only benefit and never harm each other.